WHERE LEADERSHIP BEGINS. 2E

DAN FRESCHI

PRAISE FOR
WHERE LEADERSHIP BEGINS

"*Where Leadership Begins* is an intimate discussion of leadership that builds on a personal journey of self-awareness. At the core of an authentic leader is an acute understanding of their values, goals, strengths and limitations that enable them to lead with courage, humility, and vulnerability. The combination of these used appropriately creates an authentic leader that is able to build successful teams, organizations, and lifelong relationships. Freschi takes the reader through inward self-reflection while sharing personal stories of his own leadership path. The heart of leadership is always about the people and how to effectively lead the team or organization for greater success and growth. It begins with an understanding of oneself.

Over the years, I have read many books on leadership focused on emotional intelligence, self-awareness, skills and traits. I have taken countless assessments that compared my personal attitudes and behaviors with the perception on how a specific leadership role should behave. None of these paths toward leadership growth outlined self-discovery and awareness of my authentic self as found in your book. In fact, I was recently speaking with some colleagues of how exhausted I am switching from the multiple leadership hats that I wear to recognizing my own authenticity gap in who I am versus who I think I need to be. This was a significant realization for me personally. I would like to continue further with the appendix schedules as I believe these to be invaluable exercises."

Karrie Kozlowski
CFO and Executive Finance Consultant

"Effective leadership's science-to-art ratio varies with each scenario.

In *Where Leadership Begins*, author Dan Freschi defines a viable Home Plate. (It's a fitting metaphor, Dan *breathes* baseball). The work you're holding contains a delightful blend of solid leadership concepts, uncommon sense, and in-my-own-life illustrations.

Freschi extrapolates and warmly explains:

- how applying Choice Theory (Dr. William Glasser) outperforms Control Theory and others.

- five critical leadership choices we make, how each works, and what to expect.

- why Choice Theory works so well, yielding long-term effectiveness and relational depth.

- If you're committed to effective leadership and developing team members, keep Where Leadership Begins within easy reach for frequent review!"

Phil Ransom
Writer, Communicator
VP Strategic Communications – The CID Group, LLC

"*Where Leadership Begins* was a journey of discovery of my own internal leadership strengths and weaknesses. I found myself in a state of self-reflection. Throughout each chapter, I recalled how I prepared for and responded to my own leadership experiences.

This book would be a great reference for anyone wanting to be in a leadership role. The well-thought-out ideas and experiences will prepare the reader for their own journey. As you progress through your career this book would be well served to pull off the bookshelf and read through again and again to provide a moment of self-reflection and self-evaluation."

Jeff Milne
Father of two incredible kids,
Retired Lieutenant Colonel, United States Army

"Dan has gifted the world with this great book on leadership that anyone can apply to improve themselves as a leader. He doesn't just give his opinions on effective leadership, but he artfully weaves together leadership theory with supporting studies as well as his own experiences in leading himself and others. In sharing his own stories, Dan has modeled for the reader one of the most important character skills of an effective leader — vulnerability. His stories bring the pages and leadership principles to life.

This book is not solely designed to inspire the reader to become a better leader, which it does, but more importantly, this book is designed to equip the reader to become a more effective leader. Dan even provides tools for the reader to determine their greatest areas for growth as a leader. Thank you Dan for this great resource I'll use to improve my potential to lead others well."

Blake Williams
Author and Entrepreneur

"Dan Freschi's *Where Leadership Begins* is a refreshing handbook for the leader looking to be a servant in a self-centric world. Weaving in examples from his military service and with great vulnerability, he shares the journey of a true leader — one who gains grit and strength through falling down and rising again.

Based primarily on psychiatrist Dr. William Glasser's choice theory, Freschi speaks very directly about the humility and selfless choices that an authentic leader needs to make every day. If you want to be the leader that people follow with passion and commitment, you have to choose the more difficult, yet ultimately more rewarding, path.

I have found myself quoting Freschi's thoughts in my leadership classes as they speak to the heart of the authenticity that is foundational to excellent followership."

Rhoda Strobel
GALLUP® Certified Strengths Coach, Leadership Coach

"A fascinating exploration of where leadership meets every facet of life. I can't think of anyone who wouldn't benefit from delving into the information and perspective shared here. This book applies equally to interpersonal relationships and families as it does to any work environment. Understanding and utilizing the concepts described can only lead to greater success and increased satisfaction in every realm of your life.

Taken to the next level, using choice theory instead of control theory could ripple out into society with better relationships and improved mental health across an entire population."

Theresa Balistreri
Deputy Clerk for Branch 2
Waukesha County Circuit Courts, Waukesha, Wisconsin

"I wish I had access to this well-written book to assist my day to day, play by play instructions to help me become a leader that is more self-aware, Humble, Genuine, and Courageous; all in the same paragraph of life.

I will refer back to this leadership book again and again and recommend it to many. This book can touch many careers and personal lives. It's a great book for a teenager, young and old adults that will cross over to many men and women to use as a guide and how to become a better person, mother, father and business leader. I highly recommend this book as a gift to young adults, friends, coworkers, etc. I'm not just writing this because of our relationship. I'm writing this because at the end of the day, it is what you pass on to others that is most important.

Dominic Freschi
Freschi Air Systems, LLC
A Service Experts Company

"There are books on the subject of how to be an effective manager and books on how to live an effective life, but there are only a few that mix those topics in such a way as to offer the reader a unique and unforgettable experience. Dan Fresci's *Where Leadership Begins* is one of those.

The author assumes some familiarity with the topic of management techniques in the reader, or at least an honest desire to learn them, but this book offers much more than how to be a good manager. The focus is how to be a good leader, which is a different animal.

Management techniques are focused on people and personalities and defining and communicating goals, measuring achievement, and effectively coaching those who need it.

Leadership is more about improving yourself, and gaining the trust and loyalty of the people you work with...both above and below your pay grade...and effectively leveraging that to achieve the goals you and your team thought were out of reach.

This book will teach you how to do that. Buy it. Read it. Enjoy it. Do it."

John Schlosser
Executive Consultant (retired), IBM Lab Services

"How much could we accomplish in life if we just knew the first step? Freschi shows the beginning steps of leadership in a book perfect for our times."

Scott Allen
Wisconsin State Representative
82nd Assembly District

"*Where Leadership Begins* by Dan Freschi is an excellent guidance tool for anyone invested in developing their leadership skills. Freschi makes a compelling argument for how our choices define our leadership legacy and explains how our choices influence the choices of those around us. The author shares timely insights that are helpful for those new to leadership roles and for seasoned leaders looking for a fresh perspective.

This book provides practical strategies and implementable practices that can support any reader seeking to enhance their leadership impact."

Hayward Suggs
Executive Coach – HR Thought Partner For Leadership Development, Commonquest Consulting

If you're looking for an authentic voice to share leadership perspectives from a lived experience, you will find it in this book. From military service to serving his community in post-military life, Dan Freschi shares the real and sometimes difficult circumstances that leaders find themselves in. The challenges that leaders face are many and varied, and leaders cannot always control how and when they come. What leaders can control, as Dan shares in this book, is how they choose to react to them; it is in that reaction, and in that choice, that success is found.

Duane France, MA, MBA, LPC
Author and Consultant

Where Leadership Begins
Author: Dan Freschi
Contributing Author: Jim Reed
Foreword: Duane France
Editor: Lyda Rose Haerle, John Schlosser
Cover Design, Interior Graphics, Values Cards Design: Claire E. Weber
Interior Layout: Griffin Mill

All photos courtesy of Dan Freschi

Second Edition ISBN:
978-1-957351-66-7

Published by Nico 11 Publishing & Design,
Mukwonago, Wisconsin
Michael Nicloy, Publisher
www.nico11publishing.com

Quantity and wholesale order requests can be emailed to:
mike@nico11publishing.com
or can be made by phone: 217.779.9677

N11

Be well read.

Printed in The United States of America

To everyone who chose to give me a second chance, who chose to see in me what I had not yet seen in myself, and who chose to include me in their quality worlds.

To SPC Ryan Hinojosa and 1LT Emily Perez, American Soldiers we lost too soon.

"Gardeners must know when and what to plant, but they do not control growth. They need to guard against the wind, sun, and lack of water among other forces. They also must know what can grow in their soil and what is their growing cycle, as every plot of land is slightly different from another. ... They must also know when to harvest, as well as when to let things grow."

— Richard A. Greenwald, "New Kinds of Leadership"

"Leaders must know when and how to best utilize their people, but they do not control growth. They need to guard against the organizational constraints that are detrimental among other toxic energies. They also must know what can be cultivated in their people and how they best develop, as every individual is different. They must know when they are ready to do extraordinary things and let them soar."

— Dan Freschi, *Where Leadership Begins*

chatGPT was asked, "Where does leadership begin?"

"Leadership begins with an individual's desire to take charge and guide others towards a common goal or vision. It involves taking responsibility for one's actions and inspiring and motivating others to work towards a shared objective.

Leadership can manifest itself in many different ways, and it can be exercised in various settings, including in personal relationships, in families, in communities, in schools and universities, in the workplace, and in political and social organizations.

Ultimately, leadership begins with the self, with the individual, with their choices and willingness to take on the role of leader and make a positive impact on others."

TABLE OF CONTENTS

Acknowledgements   1

Foreword by Duane France   5

Preface   13

Introduction: What is Choice Theory?   21

Chapter 1: Control Theory, Choice Theory, and Being a Leader   29

Chapter 2: Choosing To Be Self-Aware   55

Chapter 3: Choosing To Be Authentic   81

Chapter 4: Choosing To Be Humble   109

Chapter 5: Choosing To Be Vulnerable   141

Chapter 6: Choosing To Be Courageous   167

Afterword   211

Appendix 1: Defining Your Quality World   223

Appendix 2: Values Discovery   225

Appendix 3: Exploring Authenticity   229

Appendix 4: Exploring Humility   233

Appendix 5: Exploring Vulnerability   236

Appendix 6: Courageous Decision Guide   243

References   259

About EDGE   263

About the Author   261

Recommended Readings   263

Unlock Your Leadership Potential – Go Beyond the Pages!   266

ACKNOWLEDGEMENTS

Where does one begin with an acknowlededgments page? By making a choice. Over the years, many people have come and gone from my quality world. I am incredibly grateful that my quality world cup has run over with quality people, whether from the very beginning of my formation to those who have ridden alongside me for this life journey so far. I am the bearer of the consequences of my choices, but the people that have helped along the way are numerous, and I am not done living yet.

So, I'll start with **Jim Reed**. Jim is the man that put all my random thoughts, research, and writings into an assembly of words and sentences that make up this book. He immediately found my voice and has been my right-hand person throughout this process. He's been a patient partner, and I am eternally grateful for him and his family. I could not have accomplished this alone without Jim's expertise and support. If you can meet Jim, he embodies the lessons we cover in this book.

To all the **military leaders and Soldiers** I have had the honor to serve this great nation alongside. I can attest the academics have it wrong regarding today's military leadership. Their portrayal of us as autocratic leaders is so far from reality it is laughable. The following leaders and Soldiers were influential in my formation as a leader: Duane France, Al Harris, James Desjardin, Sandra Fusco, Frank Querns, General William Farmen, Donald "Doc" Washburn, Mark McCombs, Gordon Wines, Fred Crist, Sam Pena, Amanda Breslin,

Richard Drummond, Wilemina Jules, Renoir Riley, Jared "Google" Billman, John Carter, Brian Dunnaway, Wyatt Bickett, Adam Bird, Casey Bouton, Bruce Acker, Sam Burns, Jeff Strauss, Todd Bertulis, Barry Diehl, Kelly Sandifer, Gary Rains, Stephanie and Rick Markich, Eric Johnson, William McClain, Monique Palmer, Arlene Bowden, Silvino Silvino, Stonie Carlson, Harlan McKinney, Michael Langford, and so many others. I want to mention a special friend and colleague who has been through thick and thin and supported me, Jeff Milne. Jeff and I met through ROTC and have remained friends ever since, and I am incredibly grateful for him and his family. "WooHoo!"

To **Chris Schindler**, my first post-military boss, who took a chance with and chose a young, fresh, ambitious leader. After leaving the military, you gave me the first opportunity to serve the leaders of P&H Mining Equipment and Joy Mining Machinery (Joy Global). While our relationship wasn't always perfect, I still respected and appreciated you and am grateful for the opportunity. You showed me ways to succeed and steered me back when I started to veer off course. I will forever be thankful for the risk you took and the opportunities you put in front of me. Thank you.

To **Tiffany Guske**, my boss who became a thought partner who indeed became a friend. You have helped me think through many tough decisions and supported me in whichever direction I chose. I am grateful for what you saw in me, allowing me to do incredible work for a great organization. Our work together makes the organizations we work with better.

To **Meica Hatters**, you chose to say yes to the great work we did together year after year. You made our last several years of work unforgettable, memorable, and meaningful. You helped to shape and transform EDGE and our clients. You have been a fantastic friend and thought partner. I am grateful for you and the work we did together. You are missed.

To my **Dad**, I know you did your best, and I hope I have made you proud. You set an example for me that I strive to achieve every day in my way. You laid a foundation for me where I was assigned to be the architect, builder, and maintainer. Without that foundation, I would have been adrift and could have ended up in objectionable places. But, my choices led me to the present because I always wanted to make you proud and our family name, "Freschi," proud. If it weren't for you, I wouldn't be where I am today.

To my **Aunt Pam**, you were not just an aunt but an actual role model for me, my kids, and anyone else who came into your presence. You were a model of love, resilience, courage, humility, and authenticity throughout my life. I look at you and your life choices and know that I can conquer anything because, despite your physical limitations, you never used that as an excuse to stop experiencing the greatness of a life full of love and well-lived. I am forever grateful that we were in each other's quality worlds and that my kids have grown up to know one of the most influential people in the formation of my life. I honor you and thank you for everything you did, unconditionally, for us and so many others. You are truly missed.

To my kids**, Claire, Chase, and Chloe**, choose to pursue your dreams and thank you for allowing me to get after mine. Know that nothing comes easy in life, and you will gain the most satisfaction from working hard at whatever it is you want from life. Take risks and learn from every choice you make and every choice I've made. God put you into our lives to make a difference. You've made a difference in your mom's and my life, and you continue to still today. Every day is a new adventure with you. Be thankful for what God has provided you, honor your values, and always stand up for what is right and just, no matter how hard it may be. You can never go wrong with choosing to do the right thing.

To **Kecia**, we chose to partner up on this life of ours for over 20 years. We make an outstanding team. You are the team leader for Team Freschi, which keeps everything humming along at an incredible pace. Thank you for always listening and being there when I spin up crazy ideas and for helping me see them through. Your faith in God is inspiring and a model for our kids and others. I wouldn't want anyone but you by my side on this life journey. I hope you are having fun because the best is yet to come. Love you, Kid!

FOREWORD

BY DUANE FRANCE

"Hey, you're getting a new lieutenant."

There are probably few phrases in the military that generate as much potential — and dread — in the mind of a noncommissioned officer than this one: What are you going to get? The hard-charger who was told by the commander, "Take control and show them who's boss"? The one with stars in their eyes looking to make a name for themselves? Or a platoon leader who is actually going to take their time and listen to what's going on? Every new leader coming into a situation can and should assess the situation, but that doesn't always happen.

You don't really "own" anything in the military. There's not much you can call "yours," as everything is given to you — your boots, your food, your assignments, your equipment. It's like it's temporarily on loan to you. I have a locker full of army stuff in my garage, just on the off chance that someone's going to pop up in ten years looking for that equipment I didn't turn in.

That being said, Dan Freschi is one of two officers in the Army that I consider "mine." Meeting a first-time platoon leader, young and fresh out of school, is always interesting. Being a new platoon leader in the Army is a strange time: You outrank everyone in the platoon and most everyone in the company. You even outrank the senior enlisted leader, the first sergeant. That being said, exercising that authority judiciously and tactfully is critical — most new lieutenants are able to feel their way through, with support. Dan was certainly one who listened when he needed to but then led when he needed to.

If there were a direct line between Dan stepping into the role as a brand-new leader in Kaiserslautern, Germany, and the book you hold in your hands, then I was there at both ends of that line. Full of potential and promise, he was ready to go from day one. One of the first things that he said when he introduced himself to us was, "My favorite leader of all time is George S. Patton."

"Oh, one of *those*," I thought. Rip-roarin' George. I thought about George C. Scott's portrayal of Patton in the movie, all the good and the bad. Piss and vinegar. Grandstanding and self-promotion. Beating Rommel. Slapping the soldier in the medical tent. "We're going to have our hands full with this one," I said to myself. I couldn't have been more wrong.

Sure, there were times we had to discuss what was noncommissioned officer business and what was platoon leader business. One of my core tasks as a sergeant was to train and develop the soldiers under me; an officer's core task is to make the plan and set the direction. Often, training and developing required "correction" on the part of the leader, and there were formal and informal ways to do it. One tool that the NCO had to make those corrections was a counseling statement, a written record of a review of the soldier's performance. It can be meaningless or extremely important; it has the potential to become part of the soldier's permanent record. This method — a formal counseling statement — is usually reserved for noncommissioned officers.

One day, Lieutenant Freschi came in and said, "Here's a counseling statement I wrote on this soldier." We had to disabuse him of the notion that it was the platoon leader's responsibility to conduct a written counseling session with the soldiers.

Other times, though, Dan helped us understand there was not much of a difference between officer business and NCO business. I might have been brought up in the old-school way of doing things — as a private, I saw my platoon leader twice a week, first formation on Monday, last formation on Friday. He had an office at the company headquarters with the commander. When Lieutenant Freschi joined us, though, he made it obvious that he would be involved *intimately* with daily operations in the platoon.

One of the time-honored signals of designating NCO business from officer business was the phrase, "How about you go get a cup of coffee, sir?" Generally, it was well known that this meant, "Sir, we're going to have to have a conversation with someone and it would be better if you weren't here to listen to it." One day, I used the phrase, expecting it to have its typical magical effect; instead, Lieutenant Freschi stayed put. He said, "I was told that when an NCO says 'How about you get a cup of coffee,' then I need to stick around because something important is about to happen." We knew then that we were dealing with a leader who wanted to be involved, whose concern was for the welfare of those soldiers that he had the responsibility of leading.

The best attributes of George S. Patton. As you will see, Dan doesn't always hold with everything ol' George did, but he sure aimed for the positive attributes.

Dan entered into leadership at a critical time in our nation's history. The 9/11 attacks had just happened, and we were preparing for war. Everything changed in an instant; security was enhanced at all bases overseas. Our unit was responsible for setting up the processing station for all Army units transitioning into Afghanistan, and the majority of the equipment coming out of Germany passed through our unit's hands. Our new, untested leader was assuming leadership at a critical time.

Talk about being thrown into the deep end of the pool.

At the same time, leadership in the military is only one type of leadership. Many people have misconceptions about it; as I was starting my MBA program, the advisor said to me, "You're going to learn a lot in this program, because leadership in business is not like leadership in the military." I politely nodded and smiled. I have great respect for her, but she had never served in the military; she only thought she knew that military leadership was about power and control. It can be, and it often is, of course. But through my MBA program, and through what Dan tells us here, the lessons that he and I learned as military leaders can and should be applied to business. The good lessons, and the bad.

As often happens, as the military brings people together, they pull them apart. I continued on to my next duty assignment, Dan continued to lead various units, and we both deployed to combat. At different times, in different ways, we made choices to continue in, and ultimately leave, the military. Dan did so much sooner; I've watched with pleasure and pride as he's become a recognized leadership consultant, knowing how much potential he started with. I, on the other hand, continued in the military until retirement, and became a clinical mental health counselor after my career — I have the ability to speak not just on Dan's credentials as a leader, but his application of the psychological concepts of choice theory and how they apply to leadership.

Every moment of every day we have the ability to choose to build the life that we want. Often, we may not be aware of that choice. Other times, we are aware of it but "choose not to choose" and let things happen by default. Glasser's choice theory, as Dan demonstrates, is about connection, bringing people together rather than control theory.

I can think of no better definition of leadership: the ability of an individual to bring people together to achieve something great.

The choice that Dan and I made, independently, to join the military brought us together. I can look at the chain of circumstances and serendipity that led to it, and the disruption of any one of them that would have prevented it. The choice that you made in picking up this book, along with whatever circumstances and serendipity that led to it, is also a beneficial choice. Overall, what you will learn in these pages will help you understand how to become a better, more effective leader. The lessons are developed by one who was in the arena, learning the hard way — by doing. It is through Dan's doing, and providing his experience to you, and then your application of these concepts, that success will be achieved.

Duane K. L. France, MA, MBA, LPC
Sergeant First Class, U.S. Army (Retired)
Founder and Host of Head Space and Timing
www.veteranmentalhealth.com

Duane receiving the St. Christopher Medal, one of the highest honors given in the Transportation Corps.

WHERE LEADERSHIP BEGINS

PREFACE

If you're familiar with popular culture, then you have probably heard of what's known as the hero's "origin story." An origin story isn't so much about how a hero grows up, though many origin stories recount their upbringing and youth. It's more the story of transformation — when the hero evolves from the ordinary to the extraordinary. For Batman, witnessing the death of his parents changed who he was and set him on his path to becoming a crime-fighting superhero.

I believe that every leader has an origin story. (Hopefully yours is less traumatic than Batman's.) Every leader encounters a moment where they must choose a path of inspiring, challenging, and leading others to a better future. Sure, there are some who "fall up" into a leadership role, though more often than not they are more managers than true leaders.

A significant portion of my origin story — and this is one I share later in the book — occurred when I served in the U.S. Army. I was given an order that unnecessarily endangered the lives of our unit by a commanding officer more interested in personal accolades than the mission. I refused that order, which ultimately led me to leave the armed forces. It wasn't an easy decision, and to this day I still get emotional when I think about my resignation. But that started me on my own leadership journey, one in which I serve others as they become better leaders themselves.

In my career, I've encountered thousands of leaders who didn't know how to lead — leaders like my commanding officer. Many times, they are moved into a leadership role not because of their qualities as a leader but because they demonstrated technical skill or worked in the organization for a long time. Sometimes they are so long in their role that they lose their effectiveness as a leader, or struggle with engaging new generations of team members. But the most common attribute these leaders share is that they fail to *choose* to lead. They don't realize leadership is a choice. It's a skill you can develop over time. And it's work — it often requires digging deep into who you are as a person, your strengths, your weaknesses, your biases you might not even be aware of. But on the other side is growth, both personally and professionally, and a team of people who will want to work for and with you.

In the following pages, we'll discuss psychiatrist Dr. William Glasser's *choice theory* and how it underlies all our relationships, especially as leaders. We'll explore the five main choices we make as leaders — choosing to be self-aware, to be authentic, to be humble, to be vulnerable, and to be courageous — and why those choices are instrumental to our transformation as leaders. And I'll share some of my own choices that shaped my own evolution as a leader.

I'm eager to help you get started on your own journey!

IN MY OWN LIFE:

WHY WE PREPARED A SECOND EDITION —
MARIA'S STORY OF LEADERSHIP CHOICES IN ACTION

When you write a book, you can never predict who it will impact or how it might inspire others to become the best versions of themselves. As Maria's leadership journey unfolded, it became evident that the choices outlined in *Where Leadership Begins* were not isolated behaviors; they were deeply interconnected. Maria's story is a powerful example of how embracing Choice Theory and the five leadership choices can lead to meaningful change. Here is her story.

✳ ✳ ✳ ✳

Maria walked into her new role at the non-profit education organization with determination. Her mission was clear: to help high school students develop skills and find meaningful careers in the trades. Fresh from reading *Where Leadership Begins*, Maria was excited to apply the book's core choices: self-awareness, authenticity, humility, vulnerability, and courage. But her journey wasn't just about individual growth — it was about aligning her leadership with the organization's values of impact, innovation, collaboration, integrity, and partnership.

Maria's role as Vice President of Strategic Development was not just a mere title but a pivotal position in driving the organization's strategic goals forward. Her responsibilities were of utmost importance, including scaling programs, expanding partnerships, and enhancing national visibility for their work-based learning (WBL) programs. As she stepped into her new role, she was acutely aware that fostering trust, collaboration, and psychological safety would be the linchpins of her team's success and the students they served.

Mapping Values and Crafting a Leadership Philosophy

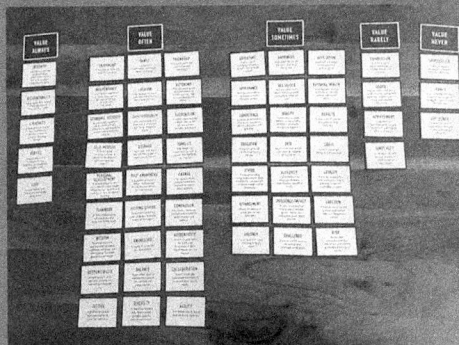

One of Maria's initial actions was to complete the Values Discovery exercise she learned from *Where Leadership Begins*. She listed her top personal values — accountability, service, creativity, grace, and integrity — and aligned them with the organization's values. The seamless alignment was striking. This harmony, where her personal values resonated with the organization's, confirmed her sense of belonging and bolstered her confidence in her leadership. It was a clear indication that she was on the right track.

Inspired, she wrote down her leadership philosophy:

"I believe that we can do well by doing good in the world. My goal as a leader is to inspire and support my team to pursue their best work. Through transparency, collaboration, and continuous improvement, I will foster a culture of empowerment and accountability."

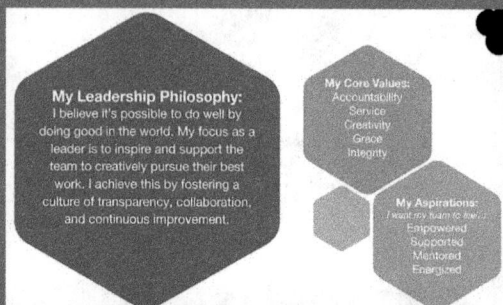

During her first team meeting, Maria shared her philosophy with her team. "I want all of you to feel empowered, supported, and energized," she said. "We'll succeed by being honest with each other, learning from mistakes, and celebrating our progress along the way." She invited her team to hold her accountable to these principles, signaling that humility and trust would be central to her leadership.

Creating a Culture of Psychological Safety

Maria knew psychological safety was essential to building a thriving team, so she took deliberate steps to embed it into the team's operations. Drawing on ideas from the Strategic Development Team Charter, she introduced rituals to foster trust and openness.

She led by example during team meetings. "Let's start with a quick reflection," she said at their weekly stand-up. "What's one challenge you faced this week, and what's one thing you're proud of?" By first sharing her own challenges — like navigating the complexities of fundraising and managing multiple priorities — she demonstrated vulnerability and allowed her team to do the same.

As weeks passed, team members began to open up about their struggles and successes. This culture of openness extended beyond meetings. One day, a team member, Jana, confided in Maria about a mistake that had cost the organization a potential partnership. Instead of assigning blame, Maria responded with empathy:

"Thank you for bringing this to my attention, Jana. Mistakes are opportunities to learn. Let's work together to determine how we can approach similar situations differently."

Her nonjudgmental response strengthened trust and showed the team that failure was a stepping stone to growth, not a cause for punishment.

Practicing Self-Awareness and Authenticity in Leadership

Maria made self-awareness a daily habit, taking a few minutes each morning to reflect on her emotional state and how it might affect her interactions. During one particularly demanding week, she became impatient with her team.

Instead of ignoring it, she acknowledged the behavior in a team check-in:

"I want to apologize for being short with any of you this week. That's not the tone I want to set, and I'm working on being more mindful of it."

Her willingness to take responsibility set the tone for the team, encouraging them to reflect on their own behaviors and remain open to feedback. Maria's authenticity showed that leadership wasn't about perfection but staying aligned with values, even when things got tough.

Her commitment to authenticity extended to external partnerships as well. During a meeting with potential funders, the board suggested shifting the focus of the WBL program to meet the donors' specific preferences. Maria knew this adjustment would compromise the organization's mission.

With courage, she respectfully pushed back: "Our mission is centered on creating equitable opportunities for all students.

Adjusting the program this way would limit access to those who need it most. I believe we can find a way to meet both your goals and ours without sacrificing our core values."

Her transparency earned the respect of the funders, and they agreed to explore solutions that aligned with the organization's mission.

Leading with Humility and Service

As a servant leader, Maria focused on empowering her team rather than directing them. She spent time mentoring junior staff, offering support and guidance to help them grow in their roles. When a new team member expressed uncertainty about taking ownership of a key project, Maria provided encouragement: "You've got this. I'll be here to support you every step of the way, but I know you're ready to lead this."

She also generously shared credit. After a successful grant proposal, she highlighted the efforts of Erica, the grant writer, during a team meeting: "Erica's dedication made this possible. Her research and writing brought our vision to life."

By putting others in the spotlight, Maria fostered a sense of ownership and pride within the team. Everyone felt seen, valued, and motivated to contribute their best work.

Demonstrating Courage in the Face of Challenges

In addition to managing her team's growth, Maria faced significant strategic challenges. One of the organization's key priorities — scaling the Wisconsin Youth Apprenticeship Program — was experiencing delays due to funding shortfalls. Maria knew the situation required tough conversations with both internal stakeholders and external partners.

Instead of avoiding the issue, she addressed it directly with the executive team. "We need to talk about how we're going to close the budget gap," she said. "It's going to take some difficult decisions, but if we act now, we can get ahead of it."

Her courage to confront challenges head-on inspired others to take action. Together, the team brainstormed new fundraising strategies, including launching an external campaign to build visibility for the WBL programs. Maria didn't shy away from the hard work — she rolled up her sleeves and worked alongside her team to implement the plan.

Bringing It All Together: Leadership in Action

Maria's self-awareness allowed her to lead with authenticity. Her humility fostered collaboration, and her vulnerability built trust within the team. Most importantly, her courage enabled her to navigate challenges with integrity.

Maria aligned her personal values with the organization's mission. By fostering psychological safety and leading with heart and strategy, Maria cultivated a thriving environment for her team and the students whose lives they impacted.

Maria wrote in her first quarterly reflection: "Leadership isn't about having all the answers. It's about making intentional daily choices — to listen, learn, serve, and act with courage. And it's about doing so with integrity, even when the path is difficult."

Her journey has only begun, but Maria knows that every step she takes — grounded in the principles of *Where Leadership Begins* — builds a foundation for lasting impact.

Stories like Maria's are why we prepared a second edition, and we hope to hear and experience your stories of transformation, too.

INTRODUCTION

WHAT IS CHOICE THEORY?

It's 6 a.m., and your alarm goes off. Do you get out of bed or hit the snooze bar?

It's 7:15 a.m., and you're running late after hitting the snooze bar (twice). Do you drive through for coffee or just get a cup at work? The coffee at work is free, but it tastes like pencil shavings.

From the moment you get out of bed to the moment you go to sleep, your day is a series of choices, one after the other. Sometimes they're mundane (*I think I'll wear my blue shirt today.*), sometimes they're not (*I'm going to quit my job to start my own business!*). Sometimes they're straightforward (*I need to stop for gas.*), sometimes they're not (*Do I want pie? What kind of pie do I want? How much is it? How many calories?*). In each case, a choice is made to achieve some measure of happiness (*I like my blue shirt.*), or at least to avoid unhappiness (*I don't want to run out of gas halfway home.*). When you think about it, the number of choices you make in one day is astounding.

Of course, your choices can impact people other than yourself.

A decision to move out from your apartment and buy a house can ripple throughout the community, affecting your landlord, your neighbors, the owner of the gas station down the street, the hardware store near your new house, your community's tax base, your representatives in government, and on and on. And all of those people are making their own choices too, some of which are influenced by the choices you made.

Making Choices in Our Relationships

While the choices we make can have far-reaching implications — implications we sometimes are never even aware of — as human beings governed by our own self-interest, we mostly concern ourselves with how our decisions impact us and the people closest to us. When you choose to purchase that first new house, you're probably less concerned about how that decision will affect the landlord than it does you (*Can we afford a mortgage?*) or your spouse (*Will we fit in with the new neighborhood?*) or child (*What will the new school be like?*). That's because you have a deeper relationship with the members of your family, and you're aware that, just as your choices affect them, their choices affect you too.

For example, think about a relationship you have with a spouse or significant other. You choose to enter this relationship willingly, as equals, and the relationship will continue to exist only for as long as both of you choose to maintain it. If you tell your spouse, "I think we should put a down payment on a house," your spouse might respond enthusiastically, potentially strengthening your relationship. If you then say "To save money for the down payment, I think we should first move in with my parents," you might find your spouse's enthusiasm a little ... tempered. This back and forth plays out in most adult relationships, and most of us quickly learn that the choices we make will prompt choices by others — choices we may or may not have wished for.

A parent-child relationship will likely have a different dynamic when it comes to authority, but the interplay in how choices affect other people remains largely the same. Children who are very young may not be able to appreciate the consequences of their decisions, and that often becomes one of the first lessons parents teach. If you've seen a parent withhold something desirable until the child says "please," you're witnessing firsthand how choices inspire new choices — the first choosing to teach a lesson in manners and respect, the second choosing to obey to get a gift. (This dynamic can work the other way too — just ask any parent who bought a toy just to appease a child in the middle of a very public tantrum.) This is an unequal relationship, as the child has no real autonomy until he or she is much older, but the push and pull as each party makes choices to get what he or she wants is readily apparent.

Choosing To Be a Leader

So, we know that people make choices all the time, choices that often inspire other people to respond with choices of their own. How does this play out in leadership?

Dwight D. Eisenhower said, "Leadership is the art of getting someone else to do something you want done because he wants to do it." If getting someone else to do something you want is all you're after, you probably have many tools at your disposal, including bribery, flattery, logic, and threats of violence or punishment. However, it's fair to ask how effective these methods are. Do they inspire people to bring their best selves to your project? Their work? Our customers?

This very issue came up under Eisenhower's leadership in World War II. In August 1943, while under the command of Supreme Allied Commander Eisenhower, General George S. Patton was in a hospital visiting injured troops during a campaign in Sicily[1]:

Then there lay a man without a scratch, no broken bones, no bleeding, who sat there in tears and said he could not take it, that his nerves had gotten to him. Patton was furious; he could not believe that such a man could serve under him. Patton told him:

Your nerves, Hell, you are just a goddamned coward, you yellow son of a bitch. Shut up that goddamn crying. I won't have these brave men here who have been shot seeing a yellow bastard sitting here crying. You're a disgrace to the Army and you're going back to the front to fight, although that's too good for you. You ought to be lined up against a wall and shot. I ought to shoot you myself right now, God damn you!

Patton then slapped the soldier a couple of times, knocking off his helmet. Patton ordered that this man be released because there was nothing wrong with him.

Patton later claimed he slapped the soldier "in hopes to make him mad and put some fight back into his heart." Whether or not that was true, it's fair to ask, would this tactic get the best results from this soldier? If someone were to do that today, would that inspire the subordinate to do his or her best work? (It's worth mentioning that "the slap" nearly got Patton court-martialed.) And, while I have immense respect for General Patton, as Duane mentioned in the foreword, we can all choose to learn from the mistakes of past leaders.

Think about the relationship a leader in a business or organization has with the people he or she leads. The employer-employee relationship is based on a voluntary suspension of autonomy, where for various reasons (a paycheck often being one) the employee is willing to be "led." On the one hand, this relationship is similar to the parent-child relationship, where one party can say "Do this or else!" and the other party will likely acquiesce to avoid punishment. On the other hand, like a relationship between spouses, participation is ultimately conditional: If the person being led feels his or her needs are not being met, they might choose to leave the relationship entirely.

In all three instances, the desired outcome is the same: You want someone you're leading to not only act a certain way, but, as Eisenhower's definition tells us, "because he wants to do it." But how do you accomplish that? How do you achieve Eisenhower's "art" of having the people you lead bring their best selves to your organization every day?

- By making choices that are informed by a deep understanding of how you see yourself and how others see you

- By making choices that are true to who you are as a leader and a person

- By making choices that seek to elevate others instead of yourself

- By making choices that pursue the best outcome even if they open you up to doubt or ridicule

- By making choices that are grounded in courage instead of fear

In short, by choosing to be a leader.

A Roadmap for the Pages Ahead

In the following pages, we're going to explore *choice theory*, a way of thinking and behaving that empowers the people you interact with, and how it contrasts with *control theory*, a way of thinking and behaving that empowers yourself. We'll then look at how choice theory influences leadership and the choices you can make to be a more effective leader:

- ***Choosing to be self-aware.*** We all have strengths and weaknesses, parts of ourselves we like and parts we would prefer stay hidden. There are even parts of ourselves *we* aren't aware of but others would instantly recognize. Choosing to become a leader starts with making a conscious choice to explore all aspects of ourselves and how they affect our personal and professional relationships.

- ***Choosing to be authentic.*** Can you be a leader and have self-doubts? Can you make a mistake? Can you admit not having the answer? When you choose to be authentic, you're willing to risk infallibility for something much more relatable and inspiring — being human.

- ***Choosing to be humble.*** Humility seems to fly in the face of what today's leadership demands. Leaders are depicted in the media as unflappable, always thinking three steps ahead, always able to adapt to the unexpected. In real life, leadership begins with actual human relationships and an understanding that they are a small but essential part of a greater objective.

- ***Choosing to be vulnerable.*** Much like humility, we don't often attribute vulnerability as a hallmark of good leadership. But if you seek to get the best out of those you lead and interact with, you need to break down the walls you or your organization constructs between leader and led. In many team sports, you'll hear of a "player's coach," one the players will "run through a brick wall for." That special kind of relationship begins with vulnerability.

- ***Choosing to be courageous.*** Underpinning all of these attributes — and so many others — is courage. I'm not talking about the courage to make a hard decision or address a large crowd, although these things are often required of leaders. But the courage to be yourself, to admit your flaws, to be willing to share your true self with those who rely on you for their livelihoods as well as those who have a more traditional view of leadership. Trust me, it's easier to play it safe — but that also can introduce its own problems and limit your effectiveness as a leader.

I'm excited that you're taking this journey with me. Let's take a look at choice theory versus control theory and where leadership *really* begins.

IN MY OWN LIFE:

WHAT ARE THESE?

Throughout this book, I have included anecdotes of my experiences to enhance the content and bring it to life. I call these, **In My Own Life** (IMOL). These can be skipped, but I encourage you to read them.

C H A P T E R ❶

CONTROL THEORY, CHOICE THEORY, AND BEING A LEADER

"Everything can be taken from a man but one thing: the last of the human freedoms — to choose one's attitude in any given set of circumstances, to choose one's own way."
— Victor Frankl

"Between stimulus and response there is a space. In that space is our power to choose our response. In our response lies our growth and our freedom."
— Steven Covey

What does leadership look like to you?

Most people would probably describe a scene straight out of Hollywood — the wise CEO / five-star general / high school basketball coach lays out his unorthodox plan, and the team, despite having their own private (or public) doubts, carries it out to perfection, defying the odds to an unexpected success. Tears flow, hugs all around.

But how do you achieve that in real life? How can you get the people you lead to not only execute your strategy, but to do so with personal passion, creativity and commitment — to put aside their own desires and to follow yours wholeheartedly?

The answer is simple: You can't.

Chalk it up to human nature — people generally don't like being told what to do all the time, and will rarely stay committed to something they're not truly passionate about. You might have some short-term success through additional motivations, such as money, awards, titles, intimidation, threats, or outright violence, but even these tend to lose effectiveness. Ask any parent of a young child how effective threats or even an allowance is over time.

However, while you can't get people to do what *you* want to do, you *can* get people to do what *they* want to do. The real question becomes, how can you align what they want with what you want?

That's where real leadership lies, and that requires an understanding of human relationships, motivation, control, and most of all choice.

Control Theory

When we are dissatisfied or miserable, our first instinct is to identify a source of that dissatisfaction — a source we can (conveniently) identify as being beyond our control. After all, we might reason, we were happy until someone else did or said X, and now we're unhappy.

But what if that source isn't someone else, but ourselves? What if we're choosing to be unhappy?

That's the question world-renowned psychiatrist Dr. William Glasser explores in his book *Choice Theory: A New Psychology of Personal Freedom*. In more than 40 years in psychiatric practice,

Glasser has found when his patients get to the root of their misery, they find it's not a spouse, a significant other, a friend, a parent, a child, or a boss that makes them unhappy — it's themselves, and the way they're choosing to respond to information others are giving them.

According to Glasser, choosing to respond to information comes down to answering one basic question, the question that each of his patients would ultimately ask him in some shape or form:

How can I figure out how to be free to live my life the way I want to live it and still get along well with the people I need?

You can immediately see the competing interests at play:

1. I want what I want.

2. There are people I want in my life, people who have their own wants (love, belonging, connection, etc.)

3. I want these people to interact with me, but without their wants getting in the way of my wants.

How we decide to resolve this (unrealistic) tension has a profound impact on our own happiness and well-being as a human, a citizen, and ultimately a leader.

My own experience backs up this observation. I've long felt that we need different people in our lives for different reasons at different times. But for these relationships to last and be mutually beneficial, there must be give and take from both parties. You must be OK with not getting what you want all the time, with making sacrifices or compromises for the people who are important to you. (In fact, I'd argue that if you're not willing to make those sacrifices and compromises, that's a sign the other person might not be important to you after all.) People who constantly take and never give anything back, or who set conditions for meaningful relationships, are emotional leeches, sucking away your energy only to fill their needs, never to offer anything of benefit in return. These people can be incredibly toxic and taxing on relationships.

Since the dawn of human existence, most people have chosen to resolve the "my want / your want" tension with what Glasser calls "external control psychology," or *control theory.* Control theory is founded on the idea that we can be happy if we can control or coerce others into behaving as we want them to. I want you to do X and not Y — if you do X, I will reward you (with a promotion, with power, with money, with sex, with love), but if you do Y, I will punish you (with termination, with withdrawal, with violence). The idea that we should punish bad behavior and reward good behavior has been around so long that it feels like common sense, and from that core reward/punish dichotomy comes the language and tactics of control. Threats. Pleading. Yelling. Manipulation. Intimidation. Violence.

The problem is, while these strategies can work in certain situations, they don't typically work over the long term, not the way we want them to, and not without a cost to ourselves. Consider this example from Glasser's book[2]:

"... using the only psychology you know, you punish your teenage son for not doing his homework by grounding him on weekends. But after you ground him, he still doesn't do his homework, and to make matters worse, you have a sullen teenager hanging around the house all weekend. After a month, you begin to think: 'Why am I doing this over and over? There must be a better way.' ... As you continue to punish your son, he and you stop talking and listening to each other. You are both miserable, you blame each other for how you feel, and he does less schoolwork than before."

This isn't to say that control theory never works — it can be very effective when the power dynamic in the relationship is one-sided, when one party relies on the other to meet his or her basic needs.

Perhaps the best example of the effectiveness in control theory is training a dog. In this case, the dog relies on you for all of its physiological, safety and social needs — food and water, shelter, companionship, etc. — and you get to determine which behaviors are rewarded (sitting on command) and which are punished (chewing on a slipper). In this instance, control theory can be very effective.

However, when it comes to human beings, the results can be far less predictable. Consider the power dynamics in the following relationships (see Figure 1):

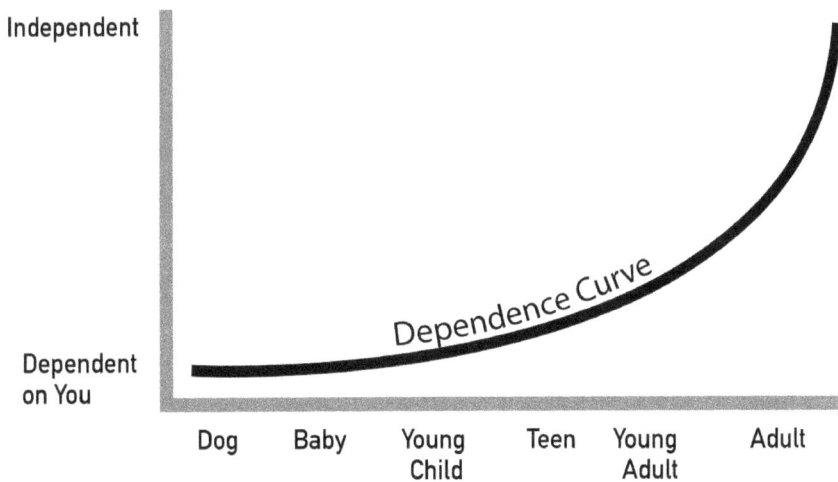

Chapter 1 Figure 1

Hopefully, with time, development, and maturity comes the judgment to live a fulfilling life independently.

The relationships on the far left of the figure are very one-sided, where pets and very young children are entirely dependent on you to meet their needs. By contrast, the ones on the far right of the figure, the relationships between older children and adults, are much more evenly split. Now, let's overlay the effectiveness of control theory in these relationships (see Figure 2):

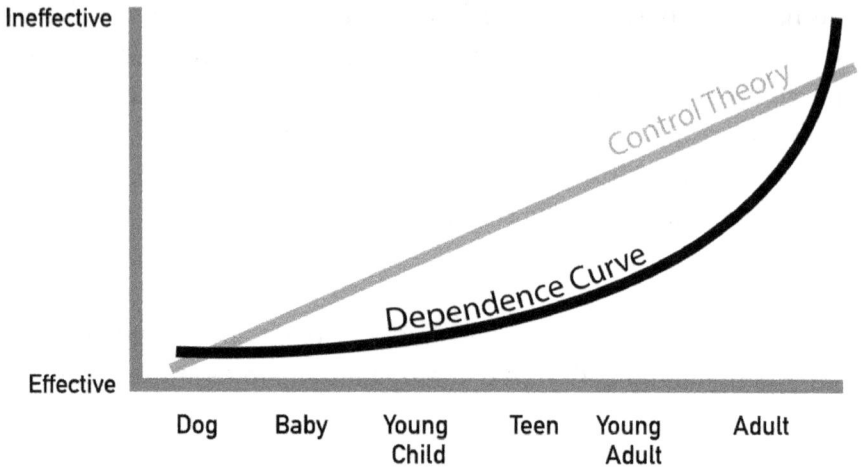

Chapter 1 Figure 2

Think about all the people you have relationships with.
The more independent they are, the less effective control theory is.

This probably feels pretty intuitive. Pets and young children can be controlled, with varying degrees of effectiveness, through reward and punishments and other tactics of coercion and control. (Though if you've witnessed a child's tantrum in a grocery store, you know that there are limits to how much even young children can be "controlled.") As children grow into preteens and teenagers, control theory becomes less and less effective, and the harder you try to "make" them do something, the more likely you're going to meet resistance — as with Glasser's homework example, or my own efforts trying to get my son to pick up his room or brush his teeth. And when you look at relationships with adults, even with additional tools of control at your disposal (money, sex, love), the tactics and language of control theory tend to be very ineffective or unrewarding. The authority to fire someone can be an effective "stick" to motivate his or her behavior, but at a cost: subpar performance, low morale, high turnover, a toxic workplace culture, unresolved conflict, in-fighting, backstabbing, corrosive politics … the list goes on.

So if control psychology doesn't work in most relationships, what choices do we have? Glasser has an answer for that as well.

Choice Theory

Glasser's experience as a psychologist led him to the development of **choice theory**. He describes it this way[3]:

"The language [of choice theory], never bossy or controlling, is always an attempt to work out the differences between people in a way that satisfies both parties. For example, open, fair and noncoercive negotiation is always the choice of people who use this new theory. They will listen, support, sustain, tolerate, and be patient with one another."

Choice theory gets away from the tactics of manipulating others and focuses instead on building or reinforcing relationships based on honesty, caring, negotiation, and a respect for the other's autonomy. It looks for solutions that satisfy both parties and seek to strengthen, rather than ignore, our most important relationships. Consider how a proponent of choice theory might handle a son refusing to do his homework[2]:

"In the case of your son, punishment — whether it's right or wrong — isn't working. Before you grounded him, he was doing some schoolwork; now he is choosing to do none. Before, you could at least talk to him; now he and you don't speak. ... If you can choose to stop controlling, even in a world based on external control, you can stop contributing to your own misery and to the misery of those you are using it with. Knowing that others need you as much as you need them, even if they are trying to control you, can help you to stop retaliating, and then things have a chance to get better.

But you can do more than stop. You can replace forcing and retaliation with negotiation. Tell your son why you are not going to punish him anymore — that your relationship is more important to you than his schoolwork and that you want to do some enjoyable things with him the way you used to. He knows you want him to do his homework; you have more than made your point. Hammering away at it is totally unproductive. If he and you can get back to being close, the chances of his doing his schoolwork and everything else you want him to do are much more likely than if you continue to be estranged."

Choice theory is appropriate in any situation where you're interacting with someone who has the capability and autonomy to make his or her own decisions. Let's look at the power dynamics figure again, this time including choice theory (see Figure 3).

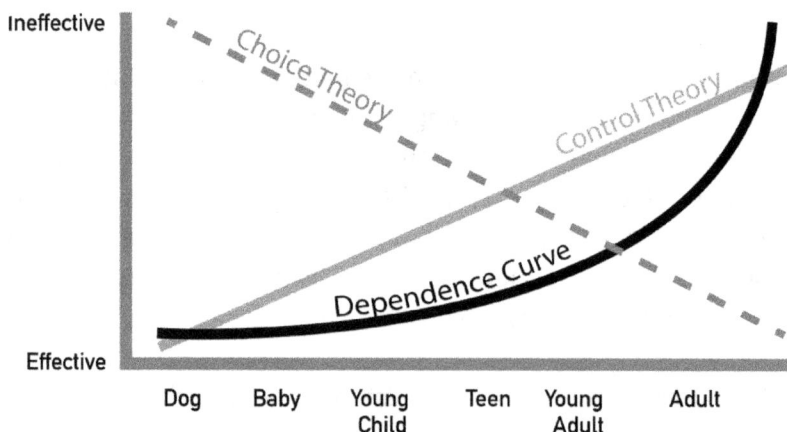

Chapter 1 Figure 3

Choice theory tends to move opposite of control theory in human relationships, especially as those with whom we have relationships become more independent and make decisions on their own.

As before, this probably makes intuitive sense. You can try reasoning with a puppy to not chew your slippers, but odds are that won't be terribly effective ("I understand that you are compelled to chew on something, but you have to respect my personal space!") Similarly, "open, fair and noncoercive negotiation" may not work with very young children who are too young to appreciate the give and take in healthy relationships. However, as young children grow into tweens and teens and their autonomy increases, it's likely they'll respond better to respectful negotiation founded on a loving relationship than they will threats or coercion. Of course, functional adult relationships are typically based on the respectful give and take of choice theory — trying to control other adults, especially those who have relatively equal power in the relationship, will likely only build resentment and ultimately withdrawal from the relationship.

And this is the catch with choice theory — it requires both parties to be invested in maintaining the relationship.

IN MY OWN LIFE:

MY MOM

I experienced this acutely in my relationship with my mother. By the time I was 12, it was clear to me that she was traveling down an unhealthy path of drugs and crime. When I was 17, my family and I gave her a choice: To go to rehab and continue to have a meaningful relationship with her family or continue down that path, which would ultimately lead to prison and separation from the rest of us. Choosing to stage an intervention was difficult for all of us, as was the prospect of essentially ending a meaningful relationship with a blood relative. However, our relationship with her was in a bad place, and for it to improve, all parties had to choose to make it a priority.

This story is concluded in the Afterword.

Most of our relationships as adults require some degree of participation and investment by all parties. Be it a friendship, a family, a marriage, or an employer—employee, leader—follower relationship, both sides need to be committed to making the relationship work. If one side decides to withdraw, then neither choice theory nor control theory will be effective. Glasser describes this commitment in terms of each person's *quality world,* and it is the foundation upon which all relationships, functional or not, are based.

The Quality World

Glasser believes that each of us create an ideal perspective on reality, called our **quality world**, in which we believe all of our needs will be satisfied and we will be happy. We lead our own lives trying to create that reality. That quality world[2]:

" ... is made up of a small group of specific pictures that portray, more than anything else we know, the best ways to satisfy one or more of our basic needs. What these pictures portray falls into three categories: (1) the people we most want to be with, (2) the things we most want to own or experience, and (3) the ideas or systems of belief that govern most of our behavior. Anytime we feel very good, we are choosing to behave so that someone, something, or some belief in the real world has come close to matching a picture of that person, thing, or belief in our quality worlds. Throughout our lives, we will be in closer contact with our quality worlds than with anything else we know."

Glasser refers to this ideal situation as "your personal Shangri-la," where you're surrounded by the archetypes of the people, things, and beliefs that make you happiest. Imagine waking up each morning to a job that is both high-paying and personally filling, a spouse whose values perfectly align with yours, surrounded by the things that would make you most content. Your quality world comprises the components of your dream life. (You can break out the elements that compose your own quality world in Appendix 1.)

When the real world syncs up with the people, things, and beliefs in our individual quality worlds, we are happy — and the more synchronization there is, the happier we become. What happens when there's a gap between how we perceive our real-world situation and our ideal world? Dissatisfaction. Frustration. Hopelessness. Depression. Sometimes even illness, be it physical or mental.

In fact, Glasser has found that this inability to reconcile the real from the ideal world is invariably the reason behind each of his patients' misery. In each case, he finds his patients feel "trapped" between (1) how they feel their relationships should go and (2) what they're experiencing in real life. Typically, they try to bridge that gap through tactics of control theory — if you would only behave this way (stop drinking, show up to work on time, respond to my emails faster, follow my plan on how to live your life), I would be happy. Such tactics of control, like we've seen above, provide unenthusiastic or even counterproductive results.

In all our meaningful adult relationships, we are in someone's quality world and they are in ours. People enter a relationship with us to have one or more of their basic needs met (such as for love, for companionship, for self-esteem, for money), and we do the same with them. Those relationships will continue so long as both parties are meeting the other's needs.

In My Own Life:

My Aunt Pam

Many factors can determine who falls into and out of your quality world. Time and distance can make a huge difference—we've all had friends from high school or college (or from the Army) who were close to us at the moment but have fallen out of our quality worlds over the years. It's not due to friction in the relationship like I've talked about with my mom, but more a natural falling out over time.

However, distance does not automatically remove people from others' quality worlds. I want to introduce you to my Aunt Pam, one of the most amazing people I have ever known.

Pam Courtney was a former Junior Olympic athlete who earned her bachelor's degree and teaching credential in 1984 from Sacramento State University. That same year, while training for the 1988 Olympics bicycling team, she was severely injured in an automobile accident, losing the use of her legs. After a difficult and challenging recovery, she persevered and became a physical education teacher despite being confined to a wheelchair as a paraplegic.

Pam, who taught students from grades 1 to 6, including those in the special education program, did not limit her classes to the usual PE program routine. She developed her own curriculum, making it easy and fun for her students to learn anatomy, physiology, dance routines, nutrition, good sportsmanship, positive character development, and leadership skills.

While this situation would have been devastating to most people, Pam made the choice to reframe it, never slowing down or stopping her from inspiring the lives of everyone she met. Her friends and family greeted her everywhere she went with love and praise. Pam was truly an all-star to her students at school, her fellow teachers, and the Sacramento community she lived in. There was never a

place she went without running into a former student.

Beyond her many personal and professional accomplishments, my Aunt Pam was in my quality world because of how she added value to me and my family. We enjoyed her company, shared the same passion for sports and baseball, and had unconditional mutual love and respect for one another. Every year, she went out of her way to spend valuable family time with us.

Despite her physical limitations, she was the only family member who consistently made the trek from California to be with us in Wisconsin. She never looked to fill the role of her sister (my mom) but instead was a quality human who truly cared for and wanted to be with us and us with her. She gave more than she took, and we believe there were mutual benefits to having her in our quality worlds.

This story is concluded in the Afterword.

But what happens when one feels his or her needs are no longer met?

"Frankly, My Dear, I Have Just Removed You From My Quality World"

Most adult relationships are forged on compromise: To meet one or more than one of my basic needs, I am willing to give up something in return (autonomy, freedom, money, etc.). However, these relationships aren't always permanent — in most cases, there are mechanisms for one to exit the relationship: A spouse might file for divorce, an employer might fire an employee, an employee might quit his or her job. In those cases, one party to the relationship had decided that their needs were no longer being satisfactorily met, not to the degree that it was worth continuing to sacrifice that portion of his or her independence. (So in response to Ann Landers' famous question, "Ask yourself: are you better off with or without him or her," the answer would be a resounding "Without.")

In those cases, the one who is breaking the relationship has likely already removed the other from his or her quality world. The relationship no longer provides the "good" feeling that accompanies having your needs met in your quality world. In short, people exercised the basic tenets of choice theory — and they chose the sacrifice involved was not worth the reward. Unfortunately, according to Glasser, once you've been removed from someone's quality world, it can be hard to get back in.

This is something I experienced not only with my mother, but in my coaching career as well.

IN MY OWN LIFE

LEADER COACHING

I was contracted to coach a leader to get better, to become more vulnerable, to rely less on his technical skills and more on his interpersonal skills. After a 360 review and several interviews and coaching sessions, we were finally starting to make headway — he was doing less technical work and more leadership work. And this behavior change was starting to be rewarded with stronger relationships with his direct reports — he was even granted access to their quality worlds by being invited to eat lunch with them and get to know them on a more personal level. He even saw a stronger relationship at home with his wife and newborn. Then the unthinkable happened, as he revealed to me in a text:

Thought I would catch up with you and give you an update on things. I left Sandmining Inc. February 1st. I'm guessing you wouldn't find that as much of a surprise but I could be wrong. The demands on my time and ethics were too much, 18-hour days and being told to lie to a federal inspector is a bridge too far. Combine that with finding out that Brock had been assuring me to my face that he was helping me but behind my back building a case to have me demoted or fired, and given his closeness with Raj his victory was almost assured.

Still looking for employment but I should hear from 2 companies this week and have 1 waiting on my answer. I thought it would interest you that in my job search this time I am putting your coaching to work on my own expectations. I am going back toward the technical side of the industry with my applications, not to say that I am abandoning my management training or experience. I am making a distinct decision to go back to companies that have a more methodical approach to their style and less of a wildcat attitude. Some of the opportunities are a combination of manager and engineer and some are pure engineering. Thankfully I have a supportive wife and a child that gets into all the things so life stays interesting.

In this leader's case, the culture of backstabbing and unethical behavior violated what was important to him, and he made the (wise) decision to remove it from his quality world. If the company president had asked him to return, it's hard to imagine him agreeing.

As a coda to this example, this leader recently reached out to me, and we talked about the decisions he had made in his career, from graduating with a bachelor's degree in mining engineering to leading a crew to planning an entirely new mine. This is what he told me:

I made all of these choices. A lesson to those looking, doubting, worrying: Never give in and never give up. I made the choice to keep learning and keep pushing. And don't forget that the stumbles are there to teach you where not to trip again. Each new choice is where my leadership began.

And the company that he left? Their questionable behavior ultimately led to their filing for bankruptcy.

To sum up the basics of control/choice theory:

- For as long as there have been human relationships, people have tried to exert control over one another.

- Ultimately, these tactics of control prove ineffective over time, especially when the people being controlled have the autonomy to break the relationship.

- Glasser's choice theory offers a new alternative: By entering and remaining in a close relationship with others and embracing tactics of respectful negotiation instead of control, we are more likely to elicit the behavior we want.

- The most important component of choice theory is we are happiest when the people, things, and ideas we interact with every day match (or come close to matching) the ideals we hold in our quality world. The better the real world matches our personal ideal world, the happier we are, and the more likely we will be to choose to participate in these relationships. The greater the distance between these ideals and their real-world counterparts, the more dissatisfied we become, and the more these real-world relationships are in peril.

So what does all this have to do with leadership?

Choosing To Be a Leader

"They will give their hands and, even, their brains to a boss.
But they will give their hearts to a leader."
— Dr. William Glasser

While the control/choice dynamic plays out in all relationships, it is perhaps most immediately evident in the workplace, where the rules of engagement are typically spelled out up front (often in contract form). Consider:

Each party can choose to enter this relationship. Employers freely choose to hire; would-be employees freely choose to accept or refuse the conditions of employment.

- Each party can choose to end the relationship, often at any time. (Though there are limitations on each side. For example, depending on the labor rules in effect for a given state, an employer may not be able to fire an employee without just cause. In addition, while an employee who signed a contract may choose to break that contract, there will likely be financial and other penalties to pay.)

- Motivations are established at the outset. An employer needs a job completed and is willing to pay a certain amount per hour/week/year to get it done. Most employees have expenses to pay for (a car, a mortgage, food, etc.) and will rely on this income to pay those expenses.

- The motivation of pay, though, often isn't enough by itself. In many instances, pay is enough of a motivator to ensure attendance but not full commitment. To get that level of performance, there typically needs to be additional, more personal motivations (a shared set of values or ideals, personal satisfaction, a passion for a particular role or field, etc.).

In a way, all of our relationships are based on this dynamic, where the "rules of engagement" are spelled out (or tacitly understood). Under these conditions, it is especially interesting to witness how control theory and choice theory are manifest.

Control Theory in the Workplace

For many people, control theory is the default leadership style in the workplace: You do what I say or you're fired. Glasser calls this kind of leadership *boss management*, and he identifies four key boss management components[2]:

1. The boss establishes the task and standards for completion, usually without input from workers.

2. The boss tells workers how work is to be done, without input from those actually doing the work.

3. The boss inspects the work. Workers are implicitly encouraged to do as little as necessary to pass inspection.

4. Any resistance from workers is met with threats of punishment or dismissal.

In this kind of environment, the boss is unlikely to get the workers' best work; rather, the workers will show up, give the minimum effort required, and leave as early as contractually required. Apathy begins to take hold — in fact, doing more than the minimum is likely going to create discord among workers[2]:

"Furthermore, in a boss-driven environment, workers who do more than they have to are ostracized by their coworkers. Since the work itself is never in the workers' quality worlds, the idea of doing quality work rarely crosses their minds. They laugh at the slogans about quality that are a fixture of many modern boss-managed workplaces. ... The specific harm of boss management is that it prevents anyone who is bossed, which means most managers and almost all workers, from putting the people above them into their quality worlds."

In their surveys, Gallup reports that 87% of employees worldwide are not engaged at work.[4] If you were a leader in your organization, is this the kind of response and performance you'd want from the men and women you led?

IN MY OWN LIFE:

LEAVING THE ARMY

Military historian Martin Van Creveld once estimated that logistics was "nine-tenths the business of war."

In early spring of 2005, shortly after the successful completion of my Captain's Career Course and a stop at Ft. Benning for Airborne School, I arrived at Ft. Hood in Texas with an assignment to literally a new unit — new in the sense that it was standing up for the first

time since 1968. At this time, the Army was going through a modular restructure that was intended to help combat units be more agile and move quickly when called upon. My new unit was one of those restructured, and when I arrived, there was not much in place as far as people or equipment — we had few soldiers to conduct our assigned mission, nor did we have many weapons or basic field equipment. We didn't even have furniture in our offices.

At the time, the U.S. Army used what was referred to as Time-Phased Force Deployment Data (TPFDD, pronounced "tip-fid") to map out large-scale deployments. If a strategic military commander requested troops and equipment, the Department of Defense would use the TPFDD to determine which units were ready and next in line to deploy. Because we were short assigned soldiers and equipment, our Unit Status Report was hovering around a 3 or 4, which meant we were not able to perform our mission.

As the Support Operations Officer, I was required to attend division-level meetings that discussed unit readiness and the TPFDD. In one such meeting, surrounded by colonels and generals, I reported our unit was non-deployable due to a lack of personnel, training, and equipment, and the forecasted dates for receiving them were extremely far out. In effect, we fell off the TPFDD — and everyone seemed OK with this determination. We were not going to be ready to deploy anytime soon and, more importantly, the DoD determined they did not have a mission for us due to our lack of readiness.

After this meeting I reported to my battalion commander that our unit had fallen off the TPFDD and the leaders were OK with our status. What happened next is one of the primary reasons I made the choice to leave the military. My battalion commander said, "We have to be a part of what's going on over there, we have to deploy, we have to get back on that list." And, within a week or so, we were informed that we were to be deployed.

To say I was alarmed was putting it mildly. We didn't have the training, we didn't have the equipment, we had no assigned mission, and sending a battalion without those things into harm's way unnecessarily was more than reckless — it was unethical.

So why was my commander so unyielding? Because when you're a leader in the Army, you "earn your stripes" by leading troops in combat. He wanted his combat patch and a performance evaluation (OER) showing he was a commander in a combat zone. He wanted a promotion. In my opinion, it was strictly a personal, political decision.

Before I continue, let me first say that I fully support the military and the mission it serves. I supported the Iraq war and believed in the evidence presented by the intelligence leaders of the time. And every day I was in Iraq, I hoped we'd find the weapons of mass destruction we went there for.

While we didn't find them, there were other noble causes that arguably were worth the blood and treasure — namely, the right of many Iraqis, especially women and Iraqis of different religions, to have their voice

heard through elections; and the capture, trial, conviction, and execution of an evil dictator, Saddam Hussein. It is also important to note that we also fought an evil enemy, perhaps the most violent and vicious as any the U.S. military had faced. The Iraqi civilians lived in debilitating fear due to the violent jihadis, al Qaeda Mujahideen, who frequently tortured, raped, and murdered anyone who misaligned with them. The U.S. military, coalition forces, and Iraqi Security Forces mission to seek out and destroy them so that Iraqis may live free was worth it, even if freedom was experienced for a short time. I refuse to believe our soldiers who died in combat did so for nothing.

As the summer approached and we were getting ready to deploy, I volunteered to deploy early to Iraq to at least help my unit find equipment and a place to live securely while in a combat zone. In

2005, from September to December, alongside my supply sergeant, I secured more than $55 million worth of equipment (such as vehicles, weapons, trucks, forklifts, toolboxes, and containers) and moved it roughly 20 miles south from Taji to our camp in Baghdad. Because no one was expecting us to arrive, I also had to secure staging areas, motor pools, and living quarters that were not ready for us, a role I received an accommodation medal for.

My battalion arrived by Christmas in 2005, with no mission and nothing to do. A long roughly three months later, we were finally

given a combat mission — a mission originally intended for a National Guard unit, one that was on the TPFDD, owned the mission objectives, and met the readiness requirements.

My commanders and immediate supervisor told them we'd take their mission, and they could sit back and do nothing.

Ultimately, we did engage in this combat mission, and I am relieved to tell you that no one in my battalion was seriously injured or killed in combat. But it left me at a moral crossroads. Do I stay in the service as I had always planned, even if it meant validating the decisions of commanders who elevated their personal political priorities over their soldiers' (and the Army's)? Or do I leave

the service, even if it meant letting bad leaders make self-serving decisions without any pushback? As an officer, I swore to protect and defend the constitution and give my soldiers the leadership they needed no matter what, but finally I decided I didn't want to be part of a decision where soldiers' lives are risked — and lost — for mindless, tragic reasons, and for leaders that were selfish not selfless.

Truthfully, it was an emotional experience when I told the battalion commander my decision. It was one of the most devastating things I had to share, and I felt I was letting down the soldiers who allowed me into their quality world of leadership. To this day, that commander is still leading troops in the Army. But I have no doubt that as hard a decision as it was, it was the right one.

This story is concluded in the Afterword.

Choice Theory in the Workplace

Through choice theory, Glasser offers an alternative to the boss management style that has become so prevalent in modern workforces. This alternative, *lead management,* is founded on four principles based on the idea that the leader cares for the people he or she is leading[2]:

1. Lead managers engage all workers in an honest, respectful and candid discussion of the quality and cost of the work.

2. The manager shows, not tells, how a job is to be completed, and is open to input from those completing the job.

3. The workers review their own work, and have the confidence and trust of their leader to complete high-quality work at the lowest-possible cost.

4. The lead manager emphasizes the perpetual goal of continuous improvement, and creates avenues for workers to share in the increased profits that come from their efforts at increased efficiency.

These four principles all center on one idea: that the only way to get high-quality work from the people you lead is by creating and participating in an open and respectful relationship with them. These four tenets speak to trust, candor, and genuine caring. In short, the leader is in the quality world of the people he or she leads, and vice versa[2]:

"Lead managers know that the core of quality is managing workers so they put the manager; each other; the work; the customers; and, in private industry, the stockholders into their quality worlds. That is, all who are involved must get close and stay close."

The question is, How do you accomplish that? How do you "get close and stay close," entering and remaining in the quality worlds of the people you lead? I believe the answer is at the heart of true leadership: You choose to lead — you make the conscious choice to be a leader.

If you're familiar with Edward Deming's Total Quality Management philosophy, this approach to fostering relationships based on trust likely rings true for you[5]:

"One of Deming's most famous anecdotes was about a foreman who didn't stop production to repair a worn-out piece of equipment, because he feared stopping production would mean missing his daily quota. Instead, he let production continue. When the machine failed, it forced the line to shut down for four days. The result was a bigger problem than what he started with."

✳ ✳ ✳ ✳

Resolution of fear comes from learning about others' perspectives and creating a working environment that empowers and equips individuals to do their job autonomously and develop themselves to progress. Creating a work environment conducive to this takes time, not just one or two meetings, to entrench the culture based on trust takes months and years of effort, consistency and dedication from leadership."

First and foremost, this book is about your choice to lead and how you get there. To lead others effectively, you must first learn to love and lead yourself and nurture a healthy relationship with who you are so you can do the same with others. That truly is where leadership begins.

Over the course of the next five chapters, I lay out the specific choices a leader must make to relate with others honestly and authentically, to enter and stay in the quality worlds of the people he or she leads. Some of these may seem obvious and some may seem counterintuitive, but I believe all of them are necessary to become an effective leader.

If you're willing to explore these choices with an open mind and commit to these principles, I promise you, you'll emerge at the end of this book a more complete and effective leader.

CHAPTER ❷

CHOOSING TO BE SELF-AWARE

"Knowing yourself is the beginning of all wisdom."
— Aristotle

Leadership, by its very nature, is interpersonal — a relationship between a leader and the people he or she leads. So, it may seem counterintuitive to think that before anything else, an effective leader must choose to look not outward but inward. As noted elsewhere[6]:

When you understand yourself, you are better able to understand and empathize with the people you lead, and in turn lead for their intrinsic motivation. Good leadership starts with self-awareness.

The truth is, before you can lead other people, you have to acknowledge that you are a human being, struggling against the human condition like everyone else. You have strengths and you have faults. There are people and processes and organizations into which you may have keen insight, and there are things that will sneak up on you and cause you to say "Boy, I did not see that coming."

And all of those human strengths and weaknesses, insight and blind spots, come into sharp relief when executing your role as a leader. In leadership development circles, this is perhaps best seen through the Johari Window.

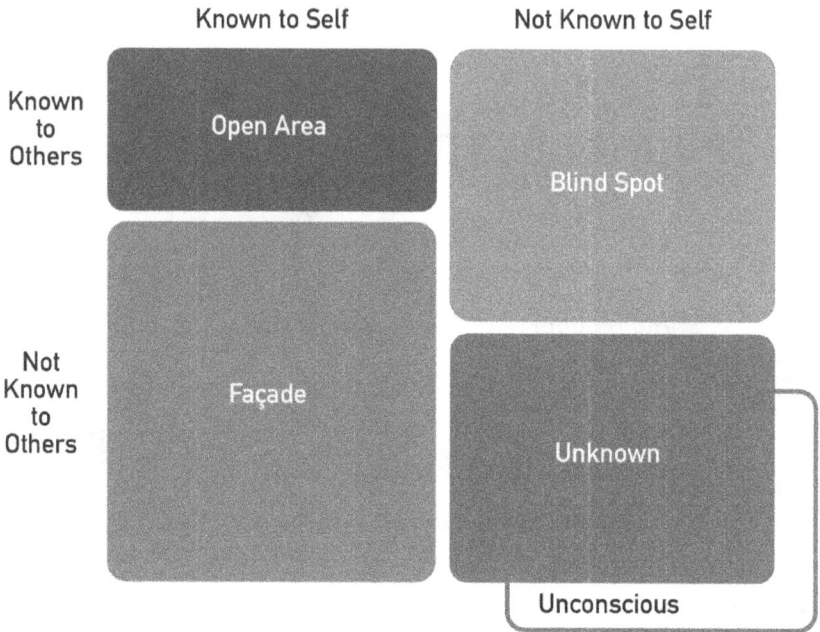

JOHARI WINDOW

	Known to Self	Not Known to Self
Known to Others	Open Area	Blind Spot
Not Known to Others	Façade	Unknown

Unconscious

Chapter 2 Figure 1

The principle behind the Johari Window is that there are things about yourself that you are aware of, and there are things others are aware of. This is true about everyone, whether or not they are leaders or aspiring leaders. The two quadrants in the column on the left depict things about yourself you already know, some of which you choose to share (upper left), some of which you choose to keep private (lower left).

What about the two quadrants in the column on the right?

These two are especially pertinent for those who wish to lead. There are elements of your personality, communication and behavior of which you are not aware, or things you think are unimportant — things others can see but you cannot (upper right) and things no one can clearly see but can still manifest in your behavior (lower right). How much are these aspects of your personality influencing your decision-making and interactions with the people you lead? How much might they be undermining your communications and relationships with others?

IN MY OWN LIFE:

TILING OVER A CRACKED FOUNDATION

This has been one of my favorite experiences as a leadership coach. One leader I worked with, whom we'll call Sally, was a national sales director for a flooring company. Even before the pandemic, her team was entirely remote: While she met frequently with each individual team member, the team members only met in person once or twice per year. While that could be a problem for some companies, the flooring company had a "hub-and-spoke" business model that didn't require a lot of interdependence among team members — and that was leaving Sally at wits' end.

"As a leader, it's my job to bring the team together," she told me on our first meeting. "But no matter what I do, I can't get them to stay engaged, work as a team, and help each other."

Sally felt it was her job to create and lead one happy sales team, and that to make that happen, she felt she needed to maintain a façade — that she herself was always happy, always in a good mood, always having the answer. These twin issues were making her miserable.

While leading a remote team can have its challenges, the problem wasn't the team — it was Sally. Specifically, it was Sally's expectations of herself and her team members, and her role as the leader of the team.

One of the first concerns we ironed out was her understanding of how her team functioned — and that started by understanding that she didn't have a team at all, not in the traditional, corporate sense of the word. The individuals she managed didn't need to interact with one another to succeed — the "spokes" that made her team run were really a series of independent, individual relationships, earning their own results. This was true even when team members shared a client: The salesperson who supplied medical-grade flooring for a hospital's surgical wing could operate entirely independently from the one who supplied restaurant-grade flooring for its cafeteria. It was a team in the sense that they shared a purpose and a skill set, but it was not one that required interdependence to achieve goals and common results.

But the real issue here was Sally's understanding of what it meant to be a leader. While wanting to "bring the team together" felt like something leaders were supposed to do, in this case it was trying to impose a leadership model that didn't fit the business structure, much like trying to fit the proverbial square peg into a round hole. The more she tried to "lead," the more frustrated she became.

Sally and I did a lot of work with DiSC and Hogan assessments to get to the heart of what she felt it meant to be a leader. Her description sounded to me a lot like a kindergarten teacher — always bigger than the moment, always having answers for everything, always positive and high-energy when interacting with her team. She felt she had to put on that façade every day, regardless of her mood or feelings or concerns (professional or personal) at the time. It was burning her out.

My advice to her was: "Hey, you really don't need to do that." Instead of trying to maintain a façade, she needed to reset her expectations and better understand and align her core values (see the Values Discovery Process in Appendix 2) and be who she really was.

Together we looked at the responses from her Hogan 360 to explore her personal Johari window and what blind spots she had. Over the course of several weeks, she gained new insight into herself and learned:

- She didn't have to do everything herself — that she could rely on the members of her team to help themselves and each other as needed.

- What her personal and professional values were and how they aligned as a leader and to the organization.

- She could set expectations for her team and hold them accountable for achieving them and still be liked.

- Her purpose as a leader and her commitment to and choice to lead.

With that feedback, we sought to increase her self-awareness and expand the Known to Others quadrant.

Ultimately, Sally realized that she sought to fix a problem (lack of teamwork) that didn't exist, and ended up creating a new one in the process. With expanding her self-awareness, coaching, and leadership exploration, she began to see the action of leadership in a different light, and to have enough trust in her team and company that she could reveal her authentic self, not who she thought her team or company wanted her to be. Today Sally is in a much healthier place, and feedback from her follow-up 360 with her bosses and direct reports is through the roof.

By turning inward and increasing your self-awareness, you can shrink these two boxes (known to self/not known to others) and improve your ability to connect with others[7]:

Research suggests that when we see ourselves clearly, we are more confident and more creative. We make sounder decisions, build stronger relationships, and communicate more effectively. We're less likely to lie, cheat, and steal. We are better workers who get more promotions. And we're more-effective leaders with more-satisfied employees and more-profitable companies.

Even a modest amount of self-reflection can foster exponential levels of self-awareness.[8] Let's take a small first step on that journey of self-discovery and explore what makes you tick.

You Are What You Think

As a human being, all of your decisions, actions, and communications are filtered and shaped by how you think (your preferences, feelings, aversions, and biases — the things that you include, or exclude, in your quality world). The Stanford Encyclopedia of Philosophy refers to these "introspectible mental states" as attitudes (beliefs, desires, evaluations, and intentions) and conscious experiences (emotions, images, and sensory experiences).[9] When we say each person is unique, that's often what we mean — not only how they behave or their personality (direct, nice, mean, fun, etc.), but how they approach a problem and how they view the world. Glasser describes it this way[2]:

All of us are aware that we live in a world we can see, hear, touch, taste, and smell. We call it the real world, or reality, and tend to assume it's the same world for all of us. But as in the fable of the Blind Men and the Elephant* (see Figure 2), no two of us perceive it the same. As difficult as this fact may be to accept, especially for those who pride themselves on their objectivity, we all perceive a great deal of reality the way we want to perceive it. … Much of what we see may be close to what others see or we couldn't get along at all, but it is not the same.

We all learn early on in life the unfortunate truth that people think and act differently than we do, and most of us have adopted one or several means of coping with this tension (with empathy, with discussion, with avoidance, with passive-aggressiveness, with a punch in the nose). In fact, the best of us are able to not only coexist with those who internalize things differently, but are able to use that different perspective to broaden their own way of thinking. However we do it, we've all learned to adapt personally to people who think differently than us — we acknowledge the difference of perspective, choose an appropriate (or inappropriate) response, and move on.

In the fable of the Blind Men and the Elephant, a group of blind men who have never before encountered an elephant are asked to describe one. One man, touching the tusks, says an elephant is smooth and hard; another man touching the ears says an elephant is long and leathery; while a third man touching the tail says an elephant is skinny with the texture of straw. While all of them are individually correct, due to their limited perspective they cannot get an accurate sense of what an elephant truly is.

The author does not recommend you recreate this experiment.

Chapter 2 Figure 2

When you're a leader, though — when you're responsible for other people in a larger organization — the way you perceive the world and act on that perception affects people way beyond yourself and people you have direct contact with.

A Human Leader of Humans

Think about the responsibilities of a leader. If you were to put these leadership responsibilities into buckets, you might group them as "How Leaders Think" and "How Leaders Act." The first bucket, How Leaders Think, would comprise your ***internal*** processes, such as decision-making, organizing, and evaluating. How Leaders Act, on the other hand, would comprise ***external*** behaviors — typically communicating the results of the first bucket to others in the organization. Those responsibility buckets might look like this:

HOW LEADERS THINK	*HOW LEADERS ACT*
Internal leadership processes:	External behaviors that people see:
Critical and strategic thinking	Building trust
Planning and organizing	Modeling ethics and integrity
Assessing and evaluating	Coaching others
Decision-making	Inspiring a shared vision
Challenging assumptions	Following through on decisions
Thinking through contingencies	Promoting innovation
Bias filtering	Rewarding behaviors

How effective you are in executing these leadership behaviors will depend in part on how well you understand yourself (i.e., your internal processes), your interactions with others, and other people's reactions to you.

How Leaders Think

Just Who Do You Think You Are?

When you lead others, you typically strive to lend a critical eye to their performance, giving them honest feedback on their strengths as well as areas for improvement. For that feedback to be valid, you always have to, as the saying goes, consider the source — and in this case, the source is you[10]:

Leaders need to ask hard questions, but first and foremost, they must pose those questions to themselves. How much are you thinking about and analyzing yourself, your own motivations, your own anxieties and your own goals? To what extent are you being honest about all of these issues? ... Taking a step back and assessing yourself honestly and critically, admitting where you have made mistakes and failed, and adjusting your course in response to those failures are truly the marks of creative leaders.

Remember, before you're a leader, you're a human being — which means that all the things that over a lifetime have shaped your personal decision-making will also inform your decision-making as a leader. To grow as a leader, you first have to look within at why you do what you do. One leadership and organizational change coach puts the benefits of self-awareness this way[11]:

If you can better understand yourself, the origins of your decisions, and the issues that affect your judgments, then, as a consequence, the identification of areas you can change and develop will become clearer.

When you look at the things that have shaped your thoughts and behavior, both as a person and as a leader, what stands out to you? What personality traits do you recognize in yourself and more readily respond to in others? What personality styles are you less comfortable with or feel more foreign to you — if someone on your team exhibits that kind of personality, what impact does it have on your relationship with that person? What effect does it have on your evaluation of the effectiveness of their choices and actions? The greater the insight into yourself, the easier it is to see how the way you think and feel can impact your relationship with others. That puts you into a position to act and foster better relationships with those you lead.

IN MY OWN LIFE:

MY INTRODUCTION TO THE ISLAMIC FAITH

One thing professionals in the counselling field try to help their patients understand is that co-existing with someone with different values usually is not the problem — it's how we deal with them that matters.

While it's true that having opposing opinions on big subjects can create friction, it's by no means a sign that you can't work together or co-exist. Some people worry that having different values or ideas to their partner and co-workers — on, say, things like religion, politics, or morality — means they're likely to run into problems in the future. Sure, it's easy to have a relationship with someone that has aligned values, but what better way to develop the critical thinking muscle than to have good discourse with a friend you respect who has a different viewpoint than you? Today's society has been polarized to such a degree that I fear public discourse has gone by the wayside. To bring it back will require lots of work, and an honest media with honest journalists doing their very best work.

During my graduate program at the University of Oklahoma, I engaged in two courses that forced me outside of my comfort zone. The first was a course on the Islamic religion, where we read an excellent book called *What Everyone Needs to Know About Islam*.[12] The second was a research course that produced a lengthy report on the country of Iraq. I enrolled in these courses because I knew at some point my job in the military would put me in contact with people of the Islamic faith, likely in Iraq.

I entered these courses not knowing much about Islam, which I assumed had a different value set and beliefs from my Christian values and beliefs. These courses and the subsequent assignments opened my eyes to learn that we value and believe in many of the same things, such as the existence of one God, prophets, angels, heaven, hell, and a Day of Judgment. And while there are many differences as well, I learned that we have common ground and can co-exist effectively and productively.

These revelations made me a more aware and effective leader when it came to my deployment to Iraq and working with people we referred to as "local nationals." It also helped me help my team better co-exist and answer questions they may have had.

It's helped me become more sensitive to and honor others' religious beliefs even after my military career. In my baseball club, we had a family that practiced the Islamic faith, and their son would miss certain events due to his family's faith practices. Having knowledge of and respect for their religious practices, I was able to turn questions into teachable moments for my son and his teammates about co-existing with others who are different from you.

What Kind of a Leader Are You?

Taking the time to look internally can also illuminate your strengths and weaknesses specifically as a leader. Consider the leaders of your organization — chances are, while they all may execute the duties and responsibilities of leadership, they do so in different ways, with their own personalities, strengths, and development areas. One may excel as a mentor, another might have extraordinary vision into the future of the industry, while a third might be an excellent communicator.

By identifying your natural style and the areas within leadership you excel at (refer back to the table on how leaders think/act), you might find there are opportunities to improve your well-roundedness as a leader, or perhaps even identify important roles in your organization that are not getting the attention they need. With self-awareness, you can more readily identify which leadership styles you're good at and which you can work on developing[13]:

We all have a default style of leadership. You may be an autocratic leader. That means that you are more of a commander than a persuader. Or you may be more of a delegator, hiring others to handle tasks and trusting them to get it done right. ... We can change our style. The combination of self-awareness and self-discipline give us the ability to change our style depending on the situation we face. *We may have a default style, but all of us can learn to adjust and take on a different style when needed.* [all italics added] We all have a starting point, and some of us are more self-aware than others. But if we don't know where to start and are not self-aware enough to know where we start, we cannot begin to lead because we are leading from nothing.

As leaders or aspiring leaders, we've likely witnessed this in our own lives. How often have we seen executives, managers, and supervisors get "stuck" in one mode of leadership, unable to adjust as the circumstances or audiences change? We've all seen companies struggle to adapt to an era of living and working through COVID-19: How many lost talented employees because of their own inflexibility? How many insisted their workers return to the office even after it became clear they could complete their responsibilities (and thrive) working from home at a much lower cost to the company? It's like General Patton all over again, whose inability or unwillingness to choose to adjust leadership styles nearly got him kicked out of the service.

By practicing introspection and self-awareness and gaining this intimate knowledge of yourself, you're better able to not only get a better sense of your own strengths and weaknesses but to see how those strengths and weaknesses play out in various facets of your professional life. That understanding, and the ability to act on it, can prove invaluable.

IN MY OWN LIFE:

THERE'S NO POWER LIKE REFERENT POWER

Referent power is commonly known as "soft power" — the ability to bring out the best in others through respect or admiration instead of hierarchical authority (or, put another way, through choice theory rather than control theory).

Here's a story one of my clients shared with me when she first experienced referent power.

Leading has never come easy for me. I was raised in a very competitive, driven family with strong values and high expectations. As a result, I've always been self-motivated — committed to my academics, my job, my hobbies, etc. Yet I seemed to lack the communication skills or confidence necessary to bring about this kind of work ethic in others. I recall feeling impossibly frustrated working in groups (whether at school or work) — they just didn't seem to have that same passion or drive. I remember thinking, "There's no way I can instill a value like this in someone else. I'll just have to do all the work myself!"

But all that changed from my experience working at the museum. I found I really connected with the organization's mission, and I wanted to bring people there. I was promoted to a supervisor position because the museum I worked in was receiving all kinds of new, positive feedback. I was building rapport with everyone who visited. When my co-workers saw regular customers come in and remember my name, or the kids who would run in and hug me because I made their time so great there, they were inspired to do the same. It felt awesome knowing that I was helping the business just by doing my best and enjoying my time there. Rather than being bitter or resistant to the "new girl" (me) getting promoted, my co-workers went out of their way to ask for my help because of the referent power I established.

This taught me that you don't necessarily have to be the loudest or the most confident in the bunch to lead — leading by example and choosing to stay true to your values can do so much.

How Leaders Act

So far we've discussed how self-awareness can reveal insights into yourself (as a human and as a leader) and how you can use that knowledge to improve your ability to flex into different leadership roles. But gaining that kind of self-knowledge can also influence how well you interact with others.

One of the key tenets of Glasser's choice philosophy is that while we can't control other people, we can control how we interact with them and, to a lesser degree, them with us[2]:

Choice theory explains that, for all practical purposes, we choose *everything* we do. ... Other people can neither make us miserable nor make us happy, unless we let them. All we get from them or give to them is information.

As we discussed in Chapter 1, this truth complicates effective leadership, where the name of the game is getting others to change their behavior even if they let us make them miserable. As a leader, one of your most important functions is to interact with the people you lead and others in your organization — to provide them information about tactical decisions, your vision, the state of the business and more. But are you aware of how you communicate, how your communication style will be read (or misread) by others, or how you read (or misread) others' communications with you?

For example, let's say you are calm by nature, and not prone to get worked up when life throws you a curve. In many of your functions as a leader, that attribute is absolutely an asset — the ability to keep a cool head and the right perspective can be invaluable.

But, what if your natural tendency toward calmness *isn't* the best response for a given situation? What if the people you lead interpret that coolness as a lack of engagement or passion, or a sign that you may be in over your head (or halfway out the door)?

In this example, the things that make you *you* could affect how others hear and internalize your communications and evaluate your effectiveness. Your choice of words, your verbal and nonverbal communication styles, how you make decisions — all of it impacts the way you interact with members of your team and others in your organization. One leader explains it this way[11]:

When you take time to consider the multitude of components that form you, and have influenced your life, there are too many change-variables to accept the notion of a static self. Culture ... family, education, environment are just a few of these. These components belong to you, and it has been your interpretation and blending of them that has become the brushstrokes on the canvas of the portrait you have created of yourself. And, of course, the picture of you that others see.

How is the way you think and act coloring "the picture of you that others see?" How are their impressions and expectations of you interfering with what you're trying to tell them? If Glasser's theory — that while we cannot make other people change, we can inspire them to change themselves — is true, then how do we create the conditions to create change? My argument is that by first looking within, you can[14]:

Create a context in which they will take up the responsibility to change themselves. And this almost always means that you need to change yourself. By changing your focus, your communication, your instructions and guidance, your facilitation and coaching. By changing the way you set the context and the boundaries, and the way you respond to resistance.

But getting a true, unbiased view of how we think and behave is no small task. It starts with knowing the right questions to ask.

What Vs. Why

When beginning your journey on self-awareness, you might assume you know what you're feeling and want to immediately skip to "Why do I think or act this way?" But when you shift your focus away from the behavior and toward the rationale behind it, you risk missing an opportunity for growth[15]:

When we examine the causes of our thoughts, feelings, and behaviors — which we often do by asking ourselves *Why?* questions — we tend to search for the easiest and most plausible answers. Generally, once we've found one or two, we stop looking. This can be the result of our innate confirmation bias, which prompts us to lean towards reasons that confirm our existing beliefs.

To develop your own self-awareness, consider focusing less on the *why* and ask a different question instead[15]:

Why questions can draw us to our limitations; *what* questions help us see our potential. *Why* questions stir up negative emotions; *what* questions keep us curious. *Why* questions trap us in our past; *what* questions help us create a better future. ... Let's say you're in a terrible mood after work one day. Asking "Why do I feel this way?" might elicit such unhelpful answers as "Because I hate Mondays!" or "Because I'm just a negative person!" Instead, if you ask "What am I feeling right now?" you could realize you're feeling overwhelmed at work, exhausted and hungry. Armed with that knowledge, you might decide to fix yourself dinner, call a friend or commit to an early bedtime. ... At times, asking *what* instead of *why* can force us to name our emotions, a process that a strong body of research has shown to be effective.

This conclusion is strongly supported by the research. Sedikides et al[16] explored the differences between *descriptive introspection* ("Do

I have [or not have] traits X and Y?") and *explanatory introspection* ("Why might I have [or not have] traits X and Y?"). They found that "explanatory introspection curtailed self-enhancement," and that "asking oneself why one might or might not possess particular traits moderates self-evaluations by reducing certainty about these traits."

In *The Limits of Introspection*, David Sze[17] examined the difficulties of identifying one's own biases, and he too recommended focusing more on the emotion and the resulting action you take than the reason behind it:

While trying to decipher the reasons behind certain behavior often leads to confabulation, focusing on our immediate emotional reactions instead may serve us better in our quest for self-knowledge, as they are often a more direct reflection of actual attitudes. In the process, we should also be open to inconsistencies between our gut feelings and our preconceived, and seemingly rational, notions.

Hixon and Swann[8] reached a similar conclusion to the why-vs.-what question in a series of social psychology experiments:

Even though a modest amount of reflection may make strong and unambiguous self cues [*sic*] accessible, focusing on why one is as one is (Experiment 3) or reflecting for a very long period of time (Experiment 4) may undermine self-insight by causing people to reflect on information that has little to do with their self-concepts … [C]*onsidering what one is should foster self-insight, whereas considering why one is as one is may prove misleading.* [all italics added]

So Now What?

"Just like a low resting heart rate is the byproduct of intense exercise, low anxiety is the byproduct of intense self-examination."
— *Naval Ravikant*

If you're looking to grow as a leader, one of the first steps you need to take is to look within, to seek insight into what is behind your behavior and thought processes. Traditionally this journey inward starts with self-reflection, asking "what" questions, journal-keeping[18], and engaging in candid conversations with reports, peers, and others. However, it can also be aided with technology: Modern-day tools like FitBit trackers, social media reviews, web browsing searches, and even computer-based assessments of video files analyzing language, voice, and facial expression can provide additional insight into how leaders think, act, and most importantly, are perceived.[19]

Let's look one more time at our Johari Window:

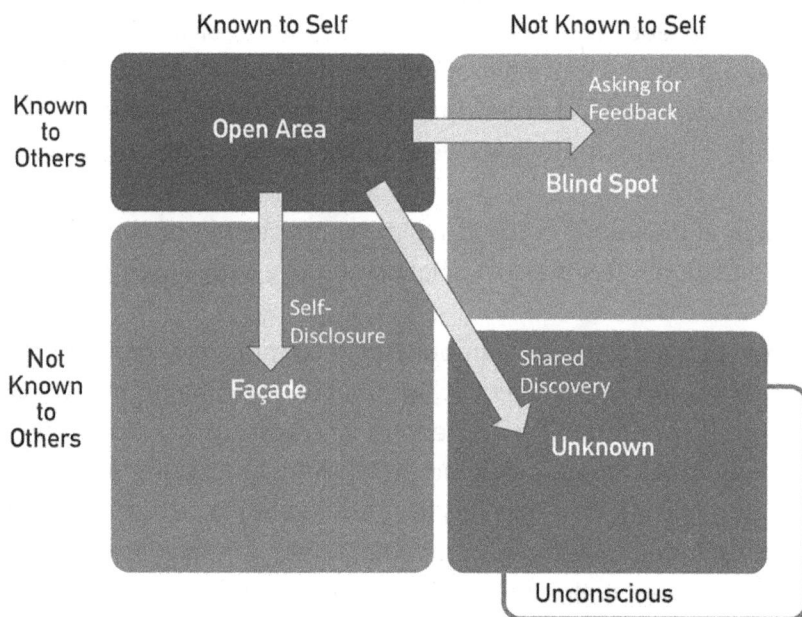

In Johari Window terms, when we focus on the What, we expand the entire open area and extend the Known to Self / Known to Others quadrants. When we ask others for feedback, that begins to shrink our blind spots or areas of behavior or decision-making that we are unaware of or unable to see. The blind spots are caused by a leader's lack of self-awareness and a failure to recognize the impact of their actions, behaviors, and decisions on others.

To expand the open area (Known to Self / Known to Others) even further, we need to tell others about ourselves through authentic self-disclosure, participate in shared discovery by engaging in dynamic interpersonal discussions uncovering new strengths and aptitudes, and finally, choosing to be vulnerable so that all the "Not Known" areas shrink.

Choosing To Be Principled

*"It ain't so much the things that people don't
know that makes trouble in this world, as it is
the things that people know that ain't so."*
— Mark Twain

There's one last thought I'd like you to consider as you take your journey toward self-awareness, and that is your values.

At their essence, your values are those principles you hold most dear. They reflect your understanding of the world and the people in it, and they drive all your behaviors, attitudes, and decisions. As we mentioned earlier in this chapter, they're a big part of what makes you *you*[20]:

Core values are traits or qualities that you consider not just worthwhile, they represent an individual's or an organization's highest priorities, deeply held beliefs, and core, fundamental driving forces. They are the heart of what your organization and its employees stand for in the world.

What principles do you live by, that you present to the world? What guides your relationships with other people, be they family and friends, coworkers, or even complete strangers? What do you believe to be true about the issues our society faces? These values influence how you take in information, how you interact with others, and how you form decisions. And just as all of us see the world through different lenses, like the blind men and the elephant, we'll each have different truths and understandings about the world and the people in it.

What your personal values are also influence who you are as a leader, and in multiple ways.

First, they set the tone of your day-to-day interactions. If you strongly believe in the merit of hard work, for example, then you're likely someone who will show up early, leave late, and appreciate when others do the same. You might also seek out and reward others who show the same commitment that you do. As a leader, that personal value of yours sets the tone for the team and the larger organization. (By the same token, you might also be more likely to reward someone who works hard but underperforms, compared to someone who overperforms but "makes it look easy." Even in our values, biases can be tricky.)

More broadly, though, your personal values can amplify or dilute your organization's values, especially in your role as a leader. When your organization's values are reinforced by your own words and actions, when you set that example and have that expectation at the top, those values flow through the entire organization's culture[21]:

In the face of turbulence and change, culture and values become the major source of continuity and coherence, of renewal and sustainability. Leaders must be institution-builders who imbue the organization with meaning that inspires today and endures tomorrow. They must find an underlying purpose and a strong set of values that serve as a basis for longer-term decisions even in the midst of volatility. They must find the common purpose and universal values that unite highly diverse people while still permitting individual identities to be expressed and enhanced. Indeed, emphasizing purpose and values helps leaders support and facilitate self-organizing networks that can respond quickly to change because they share an understanding of the right thing to do.

On the other hand, if your values are out of alignment with your organization's — imagine General Patton leading a nonprofit that sought peace through pacifism — that disconnect will likely create a misalignment with those on your team, and some will likely feel that organizational values are really just lip service[22]:

Values are also directly related to organizational success and failure, and the culture of an organization is defined by the values of the people at the top. You can have the world's most effective business strategy but, if your organizational values are not aligned, you're doomed.

This connection between a leader's personal values and the organization's values is one of the biggest drivers of success and cannot be overstated[23]:

[P]ersonal values are a more fundamental leadership attribute than the age, tenure, functional experience, and level of education in the process of how leaders influence organisations. Executive selection based on age, experience, tenure, and education to the neglect of their values ignores the invisible force that drives visible results.

Importantly, values are also what guide leaders and businesses through tough times — another lesson the pandemic has taught us. As much as COVID-19 demanded that leaders be flexible with processes, it also became apparent they needed to maintain a strong set and clear view of values to help them balance the needs of both internal and external stakeholders. Research from the Center for Creative Leadership (CCL) Labs reinforces this need to maintain a strong set of values.[24] When asked what competencies are needed for success in a post-COVID world, leaders responding to the CCL survey chose *trust, resilience, credibility,* and *integrity.* Growing as a leader requires great self-awareness and leads to being trustworthy because you have less self-orientation. Your direct reports, your team, see that you are a values-based leader and will model your example.

IN MY OWN LIFE:

GROWING UP: THE VALUES THAT MOLDED ME

There are two experiences that had a major influence on my life and my values — my service in the U.S. Army, of course, but also my time in my fraternity.

I grew up in northern California in a small town called Antioch. My father, a second-generation immigrant, grew up in the surrounding communities and provided a great blue-collar lifestyle. I'd describe him as humble but proud of his family name and what he had built over the decades in his HVAC business. My father is Catholic, we went to church every Sunday, and with the love and support of my high school girlfriend's parents, I was confirmed.

Growing up, I never really thought about values — despite the examples and evidence all around me, it wasn't something I really ever thought about. I bounced around in college from major to major trying to figure out what I really wanted to do and finally settled on criminal justice with an emphasis in law.

But something else was tugging at me. Through a college friend in the criminal justice program I was introduced to the Army ROTC, or Reserve Officer Training Corps. ROTC follows the model of developing young men and women into commissioned officers and is one of the largest producers of military officers throughout all the branches. It was there that I was first introduced to the Army Values — my first set of core values that would guide my decisions for my future.

The Army, which is great for creating acronyms and helping its soldiers remember things in threes, created the acronym LDRSHIP. Each one of those letters spells out the Army values: Loyalty, Duty, Respect, Selfless Service, Honor, Integrity, and Personal Courage.

ARMY VALUES

Loyalty: Bear true faith and allegiance to the U.S. Constitution, the Army, your unit, and other Soldiers.

Duty: Fulfill your obligations.

Respect: Treat people as they should be treated.

Selfless-Service: Put the welfare of the Nation, the Army, and your subordinates before your own.

Honor: Live up to all the Army Values.

Integrity: Do what's right, legally, and morally.

Personal Courage: Face fear, danger or adversity (physical or moral).

Soldiers enter the Army with their own values, developed over time by what they have seen, learned, and experienced. The Army superimposes its values to form the foundation of an ideal soldier's character. These values guide soldiers as they make difficult decisions in combat as well as in their daily lives. These values tell us what we need to be in every action we take. They are non-negotiable and apply to everyone all the time in every situation. They are at the core of every good soldier and demand the highest moral standard without compromise, making us all better soldiers and citizens.

Often leaders are called upon to influence their subordinates, requiring them to go beyond the normal limits of human nature. When both the leader and the follower share the same values, the Army's Values, motives are not questioned, discipline is not an issue, and both parties understand the greater significance of accomplishing the mission: preserving our country's liberty and defending the constitution of the United States of America.

Even though I am no longer in the military, I still feel strongly connected to these values and always will. The values of Loyalty, Duty, Respect, Selfless Service, Honor, Integrity, and Personal Courage — these are all values that translate to how I live my life and run my business and how I want others to perceive me.

✶ ✶ ✶ ✶

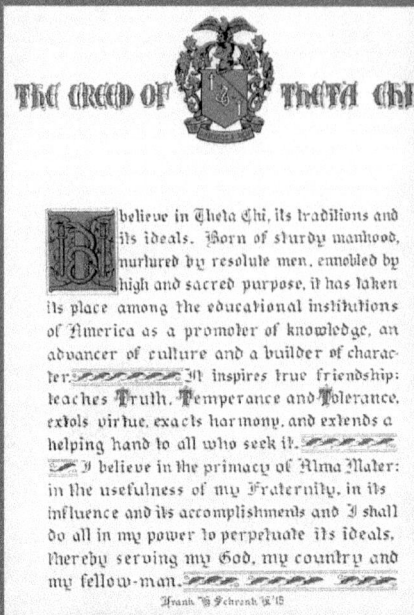

THE CREED OF THETA CHI

I believe in Theta Chi, its traditions and its ideals. Born of sturdy manhood, nurtured by resolute men, ennobled by high and sacred purpose, it has taken its place among the educational institutions of America as a promoter of knowledge, an advancer of culture and a builder of character. It inspires true friendship: teaches Truth, Temperance and Tolerance, extols virtue, exacts harmony, and extends a helping hand to all who seek it. I believe in the primacy of Alma Mater: in the usefulness of my Fraternity, in its influence and its accomplishments and I shall do all in my power to perpetuate its ideals, thereby serving my God, my country and my fellow-man.

Frank H Schrenk K'15

At around the same time I was learning the Army Values, I was At around the same time, I was starting the process of rushing a fraternity. I had attempted rushing a fraternity my freshman year but found it wasn't the right fit for me for many reasons. After waiting a few years, I revisited the idea with a new fraternity, Theta Chi. Theta Chi was a match for me and still today is an important part of who I am.

What struck me were the actual words in the creed:

I believe in Theta Chi, its traditions and its ideals. Born of sturdy manhood, nurtured by resolute men, ennobled by high and sacred purpose, it has taken its place among the educational institutions of America as a promoter of knowledge, an advancer of culture, and a builder of character.

It inspires true friendship; teaches Truth, Temperance, and Tolerance, extols virtue, exacts harmony, and extends a helping hand to all who seek it.

I believe in the primacy of Alma Mater; in the usefulness of my Fraternity, in its influence and its accomplishments and I shall do all in my power to perpetuate its ideals, thereby serving my God, my country, and my fellow-man.

Leadership is a team sport, and a leader must inspire truth, temperance, and tolerance. Extend helping hands to all who seek it, advance culture, promote harmony, and help to build and reinforce one's character. Leadership serves a higher purpose for all who choose to do it well.

So how do values tie back into self-awareness? Consider what Kraemer wrote about values-based leadership[25]:

[Y]our leadership must be rooted in who you are and what matters most to you. When you truly know yourself and what you stand for, it is much easier to know what to do in any situation. It always comes down to doing the right thing and doing it to the best of your ability.

If you're truly to lead in your organization, you — and those you have relationships with — need to know exactly where you stand. That understanding leads to consistency, and that consistency leads to trust. As you explore the two tracks of self-awareness — what you know about yourself, what others know about you — it's also worth asking yourself: What values do you prioritize?

This isn't a one-time journey. Values are not static — as you grow and mature over time, your values can evolve with you. Sometimes they will be in conflict, and you have to prioritize one value over another. But by developing your self-awareness, you can learn about why you think and act the way you do, your values and how firmly you hold them, and how it all colors your decision-making and interactions with others. In the next chapter, we'll explore what happens when leaders accept — or reject — this new understanding.

Just like the first step in an effective weight loss program is often onto the scale,[26] the first step to effectively growing your self-awareness is examining what you value. If you received the Values Discovery Cards accompanying this book, head on over to Appendix 2 and start the Values Discovery Process. If you did not, you can visit our website and purchase a physical set or download a digital set:

whereleadershipbegins.com

or scan here:

C H A P T E R ❸

CHOOSING TO BE AUTHENTIC

"Authenticity is a virtue. But just as you can have
too little authenticity, you can also have too much."
— Adam Grant

Choosing to be authentic? Authenticity is a choice?

It is — and it's a vital one if you're to be an effective leader. Over the last 20 years, there has been a movement within leadership development that has emphasized the importance of authenticity, with Bill George's seminal book *Authentic Leadership: Rediscovering the Secrets to Creating Lasting Value* leading the charge. However, despite all the press and discussion over authentic leadership, there is still confusion about what it means to be an authentic leader. In this chapter we're going to look at what leaders are getting wrong about authenticity and why it's a lot harder, and requires a lot more courage, than we think.

The Search for Authentic Leaders

Imagine you're a finalist for a position on an executive team, and the CEO tells you that the most important trait they're looking for in a leader is authenticity. What do you think that means? What traits do you think they're looking for? Before you answer "Just being true to myself," consider these three examples of team leaders who chose authenticity[27]:

- Meet Cynthia, a general manager in a health care organization. Her promotion into that role increased her direct reports 10-fold and expanded the range of businesses she oversaw — and she felt a little shaky about making such a big leap. A strong believer in transparent, collaborative leadership, she bared her soul to her new employees: "I want to do this job," she said, "but it's scary, and I need your help." Her candor backfired; she lost credibility with people who wanted and needed a confident leader to take charge.

- Anne, a senior manager at a transportation company, had doubled revenue and fundamentally redesigned core processes in her unit. Despite her obvious accomplishments, however, her boss didn't consider her an inspirational leader. Anne also knew she was not communicating effectively in her role as a board member of the parent company. The chairman, a broad-brush thinker, often became impatient with her detail orientation. His feedback to her was "step up, do the vision thing." But to Anne that seemed like valuing form over substance. "For me, it is manipulation," she told me in an interview. "I can do the storytelling too, but I refuse to play on people's emotions. If the string-pulling is too obvious, I can't make myself do it."

- Let's look at Jacob, a food company production manager whose direct reports gave him low marks in a 360 review on emotional intelligence, team building, and empowering others. One team member wrote that it was hard for Jacob to accept criticism. Another remarked that after an angry outburst, he'd suddenly make a joke as if nothing had happened. ... Jacob acknowledged that this was not the first time he'd received such criticism (some colleagues and subordinates had made similar comments a few years earlier). "I thought I'd changed my approach," he reflected, "but I haven't really changed so much since the last time." However, he quickly rationalized his behavior to his boss: "Sometimes you have to be tough in order to deliver results, and people don't like it," he said. "You have to accept that as part of the job description."

In each of these three instances, these leaders struggled with reconciling who they were as people with the demands of leadership — or, more accurately, what they *understood* being a leader demanded of them. They felt adopting a mask would ultimately lead to quicker acceptance as a leader and better outcomes with their reports. While this motivation is certainly understandable, it certainly could backfire[28]:

In our research we found two ways in which leaders use a mask. One is to conceal perceived inadequacies and flaws to preserve the polished façade we have come to expect of "great" leaders. The other, more subtle way is to adopt a certain persona at work that the leader feels is necessary for success. Both uses undermine trust and effectiveness. They also create inner conflict, as leaders struggle to align their work and home lives. By dropping the mask, a leader can craft a more meaningful and congruent identity, which enhances relationships and business outcomes.

Choosing to be authentic may sound like it's easy. Far from it — not when it leads you to put your feelings, values, and communication styles ahead of your team's. Leadership, authentic or otherwise, will always be founded on a relationship between yourself and the people you lead. If you're going to maintain and build that relationship — to remain in your team's "quality worlds" — you need to establish trust and share yourself with your team while remaining a leader. Others' trust in you grows when you are true to yourself, and that trust makes it possible to accomplish things together. And when we are authentic as leaders, our followers will find respite in being authentic themselves. Excellence is contagious.

Before you can start leading with authenticity, though, we should first talk about what authenticity means as a leader.

What Authentic Leadership Is

According to Walumbwa et al[29, 110]:

[A]uthentic leadership represents the extent to which a leader is aware of and exhibits patterns of openness and clarity in his/her behavior toward others by sharing the information needed to make decisions, accepting others' inputs, and disclosing his/her personal values, motives, and sentiments in a manner that enables followers to more accurately assess the competence and morality of the leader's actions.

That's a lot to take in. To me, the important part of that definition is the "patterns of openness and clarity," what one might call a "consistency between a person's internal values and his/her external expressions."[30] Trilling shared that external expression is the sincerity of who we are through meeting our obligations and fulfilling our responsibilities.[31] Authentic leadership is about easing the tension between your inner self and outer self, leading your reports and organization and creating necessary change, but in a way that sincerely reflects who you are as a leader and a person in terms of values, behaviors, and even emotions.[32] It's interacting and building trust with people inside and outside of your organization in a way that is an honest and sincere reflection of who you are as a person.

IN MY OWN LIFE:

BETTY, SIDNEY, AND WHY WE TALK ABOUT AUTHENTICITY

The authenticity gap, when you think about it, is a problem of our own making. Consciously or otherwise, we evaluate a leadership opportunity in front of us, and either we find ourselves deficient or assume that others will (and potentially take that opportunity from us). So we dress the part, use the same words, and "prove" that we're leaders by — paradoxically — trying to blend in as much as possible.

Sometimes, though — as the recent passing of Betty White and Sidney Poitier remind us — the authenticity gap is imposed by events going on outside yourself.

Within one week of each other, the world lost two premier acting talents: Betty White, a seven-time Emmy award winner, and Sidney Poitier, the first Black actor to win the Academy Award for Best Actor. We also lost two leaders who weren't afraid to be proudly authentic when the rest of the world told them to sit down.

Betty White's entertainment career first started in the late 1940s, a time when women were expected to marry young and raise a large family rather than pursue careers outside the home. (In fact, she is said to have divorced her second husband because he wanted a stay-at-home wife and she wanted to follow her career in radio and television.) Soon after, in 1954, she was criticized for having Arthur Duncan, a Black tap dancer, perform on her national variety show and risked the cancellation of her show. Her response: "Live with it."

Before he became a famous actor, Sidney Poitier worked as a deliveryman. As he recalled in an NPR interview, at one point he went to deliver a package to a white woman's home. She opened the door, screamed at him, and slammed the door in his face. As if that weren't traumatizing enough, soon after the KKK showed up at his house. Despite it all, he was able to persevere in a society that did not treat him as an equal. When asked to reflect on his career, he responded "I am going to be who I am, regardless of what I'm in the face of."[33]

In both of these cases, being authentic brought risk, both professional and even personal. Here's how the Center for Creative Leadership podcasts thought about it:

Holding onto that authenticity, in the face of all that would be dangerous and treacherous about it, seems so unique. ... As a leader, if you're listening and thinking about impact and legacy and opening the door for others and holding it open, it's maybe modeling that authenticity. Even when there's a risk for it.[33]

Can authentic be risky? Sure, especially because, as the hosts discuss, "authentic" doesn't mean "perfect." It takes courage and trust. But then again, doesn't leadership?

An illustration might help. This is you:

Chapter 3 Figure 1

In this circle are the things that define your character and your identity: your values, your intentions, your personality, your fears, your beliefs, your biases, all the things you believe in. If you are a self-aware leader, you probably have a good handle on these characteristics, both good and bad. This is the *you* you think you are.

Now let's add another layer:

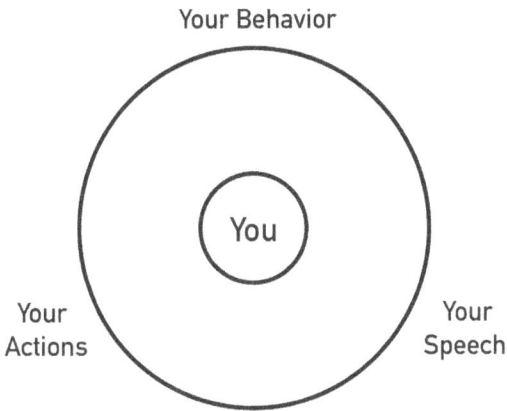

Your Behavior

You

Your
Actions

Your
Speech

Chapter 3 Figure 2

The outer ring is your behavior, speech, and actions — the way you appear to the outside world. This is how others experience you and see your reputation.

Now look at the space between the inner and outer rings:

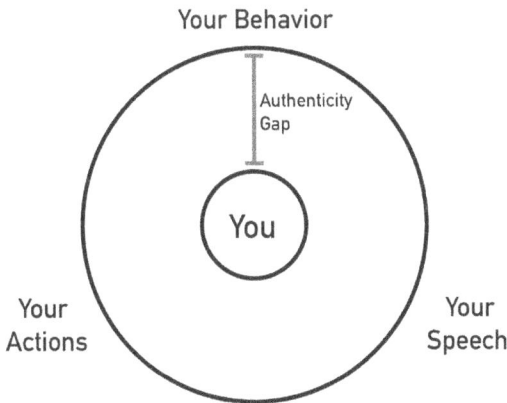

Your Behavior

Authenticity
Gap

You

Your
Actions

Your
Speech

Chapter 3 Figure 3

That gap between your feelings and identity at your core and how people perceive you and your reputation could be called an "authenticity gap." The smaller the gap, the more authentic and sincere others perceive you to be. The larger the gap, the more you have to keep up the facade of who you are not, which can be emotionally, cognitively, and physically exhausting.

Ideally, your reputation, actions, and behaviors as a leader directly reflect your inner self, identity, personality, and core beliefs, leading to only a small authenticity gap. However, on the journey to becoming a leader, it's easy to lose yourself in pursuit of how people expect a leader to behave — expectations that you yourself might have, or external pressure such as how your organization specifically lays out (perhaps even in writing) how to behave. In either case, the thinking often follows like this:

1. "Leaders behave a certain way."
2. "I want to be seen as a leader."
3. "I need to behave this way."

Sometimes the image of a leader we subscribe to might look something like this: stiff, emotionless, unsmiling, aloof. Maybe wearing a suit or pantsuit. Not immediately willing to share personal information and events outside of small talk. *Certainly* not willing to share doubts or concerns.

While looking the part may be politically expedient, people — especially the members on your own team — will quickly realize when someone is insincere and trying to "fake it until they make it" or build a wall between leader and team. That undercuts their trust, their confidence in your leadership ability, and the cohesiveness of the team. Robinson and O'Dea put it this way[34]:

The problem is that by 'acting the role' of leader, those around them often feel like they're being lied to or deceived. Then leaders are stunned when their employees don't like them, don't trust them and end up leaving. But if individuals can remain authentic in their leadership approach, they can bring their whole self to work while still being effective, productive and inspiring leaders.

Refining the Authenticity Gap

Authenticity is not about playing a role, but it is also not about ignoring the reality that how we show up matters. It is about learning to express who we truly are in ways that others can trust and follow.

Many leaders believe that authenticity means rejecting anything that feels rehearsed. They equate sincerity with spontaneity and see managing impressions as dishonest. In reality, leadership is not an unfiltered display of who we are; it is an intentional expression of our best, most authentic, aligned self.

Between being brutally honest and overly guarded, there is a space where effective leadership resides. Impression management is often mistaken for manipulation, but it is actually better viewed as purposeful alignment. Strong leaders do not neglect impression management; they refine it. They curate how they show up so that their words, tone, and actions mirror their core values while also addressing the needs of those they lead.

Curating isn't about pretending. It's about aligning our beliefs with what others need to experience from us to build trust and inspire followership. A leader's presence, tone, and emotional discipline are powerful ways to communicate values, often more impactful than words.

Recent critics have challenged traditional ideas of authentic leadership and offer important insights that strengthen our understanding of what authenticity really demands. Tomas Chamorro-Premuzic[118] argues that authenticity has become a "feel-good theory," too often reduced to personal expression rather than to leadership performance. Jeffrey Pfeffer[119] warns that being "true to yourself" can conflict with the practical realities of influence and responsibility, noting that leadership requires adaptation and disciplined self-regulation. Dennis Tourish[120] cautions that theories of authentic leadership risk idealizing human nature and overlooking moral complexity, reminding us that authenticity must account for both light and shadow.

These critiques point to a shared truth: authenticity without discernment becomes self-indulgence. Authenticity is not about revealing every part of ourselves, but about exercising judgment: choosing which parts of ourselves to bring forward in service to others and the mission.

Impression management, when guided by integrity, becomes a skill of stewardship. It is how leaders manage the perceptions that allow their authenticity to be recognized. Every leader shapes impressions, whether intentionally or not. The question is whether those impressions are consistent with what you stand for.

When your outward presence aligns with your inward principles, you close the authenticity gap not by removing performance, but by performing with integrity. Leaders who do this well are not putting on a show. They are communicating deliberately and with purpose. Measured authenticity balances sincerity with strategic awareness, which means being mindful of how your actions and words will be perceived and their potential impact on others. This marks the maturity of authentic leadership.

Authentic leaders channel their authenticity with purpose and clarity, ensuring their actions and words align with their values and principles.

Authentic leaders don't fake it. They focus it.

Consider this counter-example that reflects the experiences of one of my coaching clients to the letter[35]:

A seasoned leader was meeting with her team to discuss a decline in sales that needs to be turned around before quarter-end. She knows everything there is to know about the clients, competitors, and products. But somewhere in the back of her mind, she's thinking, "None of you is pulling your weight. I'm carrying all of you. But I need you to execute or I'm going to look bad in front of my boss and senior leaders and miss my year-end bonus." Meanwhile, on the outside, she's explaining, "Yes, the market is a challenge, but our clients need our product. Our sales team is top-notch. Let's go out there and hit one out of the park." ... The gap between what the manager is authentically thinking or feeling and what the manager is publicly telling her team undermines and distorts everything she is trying to accomplish.

(If you were in the room with her and had known her at all, you would see that her tone, expression, and energy are at odds with her words.)

The sense that a leader is being disingenuous or untruthful can severely undermine the relationship between a leader and those he or she leads. We discussed previously that people choose to be led, to sacrifice some of their personal autonomy for a greater cause. For most people, there is an implicit understanding in this relationship: "I will give you my best effort if I feel you have my best interests at heart." As we see with the leader above, if a team senses a disconnect between a leader's words and actions, they — lacking the benefit of access to senior leadership's motivations or additional context — will question whether they are being entrusted with the truth, and the leadership relationship becomes severely undermined.

And this is the crucial idea behind authentic leadership — that while developing authenticity is a reflective, inward action, its value lies in the relationships it allows you to build with others. Consider this diagram from Avolio et al.[36]:

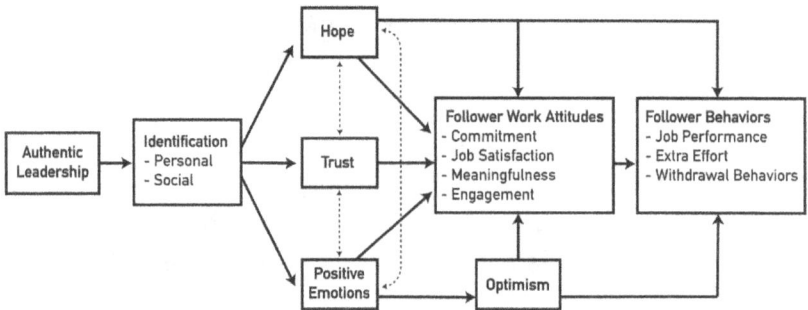

Chapter 3 Figure 4

While admittedly, this may appear to be a complicated flowchart, the essence of it is authentic leadership will help you develop hope, trust, and positive emotions among the people you lead, emotions that, in turn, will lead to engagement, commitment, discretionary effort, and job performance.

Demonstrating authenticity is not about creating a false picture of yourself but recognizing genuine aspects of yourself that should show up and be seen by others — but are hidden (as discussed in Chapter 2 about the Johari Window).

Essentially, you are working to match who you are inside with your external reputation. As the authors state[36]:

Our proposed model … recognizes that although authentic leadership is important, it is not sufficient to achieve desired goals. As shown, there is a process linking authentic leadership to followers' attitudes and behaviors.

When a followers' attitudes and behaviors such as discretionary efforts, engagement behaviors, and high job performance are influenced through authenticity it will also open up the followers' quality world.

The process of "linking authentic leadership to followers' attitudes and behaviors" is one way to open up the quality worlds of the people you lead and allow you in and stay.

So now that we understand the value of authentic leadership, let's dive deeper into authentic leadership in practice.

So What Does Authentic Leadership Look Like?

Some research suggests that authentic leaders tend to exhibit three essential behaviors.[34] They:

- Demonstrate behaviors which enable you to trust in them all the time

- Take ownership when they have made a mistake and share responsibility for any mistake

- Show the necessary courage to push further up the leadership chain, to question current status quo or defend their people or processes

These behaviors build credibility, humility, sincerity, and genuine concern for those you lead, fostering a foundation of psychological safety. Rather than striving for perfection, which can create distance, embracing your humanness—acknowledging mistakes, even failures, and openly taking responsibility—goes much further in earning the trust of your team. When leaders demonstrate vulnerability, they also demonstrate inclusion and learner safety.[114] They signal to team members that it's safe to show up as their authentic selves, imperfections and all. This openness enhances authenticity and breaks down barriers, inviting team members to engage in meaningful, honest relationships.

Such genuine relationships are why people commit themselves to an organization and a leader. By creating psychologically safe environments where authenticity and vulnerability are prioritized, leaders inspire commitment in ways that manipulation, threats, or traditional "carrot and stick" strategies cannot. Authentic leadership empowers individuals to feel valued and understood, motivating them to contribute fully and enthusiastically. When people feel safe expressing their thoughts and taking risks, they are more likely to be innovative, resilient, and invested in the organization's success.

To be clear: Authentic leadership takes courage. It is easier to maintain distance, to let the natural "walls" between leader and team keep others at arm's length. Choosing to be authentic, to narrowing the gap between who we see ourselves to be and how we behave and establishing a relationship with the people we lead, risks rejection. Therefore, authenticity is rooted in trust — first with yourself, then in the context or environment. Glasser expresses it this way[2]:

Most of us are reluctant to share what is in our quality worlds, even with people we are close to, because we are afraid they may not support what we want — that they may criticize or ridicule what is so important to us. We know we would choose to feel hurt, angry, or both, if they did criticize or ridicule.

That fear exists, to some extent, in all our relationships, personal and professional, and can undermine our ability to serve as leaders[37]:

Why does being our real-self cause fear? Fear of being judged or criticized, concern over being disliked or shut-out, and worry about overshadowing others can all be reasons for people to be afraid and to hide whom they believe themselves to really be.

What is the fear of authenticity? It is the fear of showing people who you really are. Maybe for a long time you've hidden behind sarcasm or inauthentic actions that distracted people from seeing the real you. Sometimes people act smaller than they are. Sometimes people remain the class clowns they were in high school. It is not uncommon for people to present themselves as other than who they really are or who they want to be.

When I speak to leaders from for-profit and non-profit businesses alike, I feel I have a good sense of who is being authentic and genuine and who is not. I believe this comes from recognizing my own authenticity mask, which is rooted in cynicism. Some people call cynicism "quick-wittedness." However, looking back, my cynicism was a shield to keep people from seeing who *I* was while I played out who I thought they wanted me to be. (Ironically, we often overstate, even to ourselves, how much others are paying attention to that image we so carefully construct — more often than not, they are much more worried about themselves and what *we* think of *them*.) Whatever the mask, the real, authentic person is there, waiting to be seen, heard, and understood. It takes courage to narrow the authenticity gap — choosing authenticity can be both a fearful choice and a courageous, life-enhancing choice.

It's certainly easier to stay aloof and follow the model of how we expect leaders to behave. But we know that remaining distant does not inspire others to be passionate about their work, to give their best effort, or even to stay loyal to the organization. Only a true, authentic relationship between leader and team can do that[38]:

Had I approached the role as a know-it-all new manager, I would have been dogged by the image I had to uphold rather than leveraging my strengths to buy time to work on my areas for improvement. My team supported me because they got the real me, not some impostor, and in the end, my first manager role was a success that led me to increased responsibilities and bigger roles in the future.

But what about the problems Cynthia, Anne, and Jacob were experiencing? Using what we know about authenticity, let's take a closer look at their problems with leadership.

Cynthia

In the first example, Cynthia confessed to her team that she was in over her head. She was certainly being true to herself, but was she leading? It's worth reviewing the message she had for her team:

"I want to do this job," she said, *"but it's scary, and I need your help."*

If you were a member of her team, how would you feel about this message? Right away, of course, you would probably question her competence in leading as she seems in over her head. But this message also expresses no concern for her team and how they are going to thrive under her leadership, nor does it speak to the common purpose of their team or the goals of the larger organization. In essence, she's asking them to commit to and engage in a relationship where her needs are all that matter. Especially as a new leader, that's not likely to gain her acceptance into their quality worlds.

In addition, while Cynthia is being authentic, she is forgetting that her role as a leader does set her apart from the team — she was asked to lead because she is believed to have the experience, judgment, and big-picture-thinking to do it. The "sweet spot" between authentic and overly familiar has been described this way[27]:

A deeper-seated issue is finding the right mix of distance and closeness in an unfamiliar situation. Stanford psychologist Deborah Gruenfeld describes this as managing the tension between authority and approachability. To be authoritative, you privilege your knowledge, experience, and expertise over the team's, maintaining a measure of distance. To be approachable, you emphasize your relationships with people, their input, and their perspective, and you lead with empathy and warmth.

It's a tightrope, for sure, but leading with authenticity still requires leading.

Let's now look at Anne's example.

Anne

In a way, Anne is the opposite situation from Cynthia — highly detail-oriented and successful, she struggles to express a vision that could inspire her team and clarify their purpose. This is a common struggle among new leaders, especially those who aren't overly gregarious and prefer to "let their work stand for itself." In this case, authenticity is being used as a crutch: "If I feel I have to sell myself and the merits of my work to others, then I'm not being me."

Communicating a vision and rallying others behind it is one of the most important functions of leadership, and what distinguishes leadership from management. In many cases, it becomes a matter of the new leader understanding the value they bring to the organization and taking a bigger-picture perspective[27]:

Until we see career advancement as a way of extending our reach and increasing our impact in the organization — a collective win, not just a selfish pursuit — we have trouble feeling authentic when touting our strengths to influential people. ... Research shows, however, that this hesitancy disappears as people gain experience and become more certain of the value they bring.

It's also worth examining Anne's conundrum through Glasser's lens of leadership relationships. The request that she do "the vision thing" may not be a capricious comment by the chairman. When you're leading an organization through change, the people you lead will want to know you have a strategy for success and you have their best interests at heart. Anne has reason to be concerned: if she tries to do "string-pulling," as she phrases it, she will almost certainly do it unconvincingly. The challenge for her is to inspire and motivate in a way that is believable and authentic to her.

Let's finish with Jacob.

Jacob

Jacob seems to struggle with criticism and is prone to angry outbursts; however, when confronted with this behavior, he doubles down, telling his boss, "Sometimes you have to be tough in order to deliver results, and people don't like it." Jacob's style of leadership clearly reflects his personality, but judging by his 360 evaluation responses, it doesn't seem to be effective.

Of course, his behavior in no way fits Glasser's model of "respectful negotiation" — his evaluations should serve as alarm bells that he is falling out of his team's quality worlds. Jacob's behavior can be compared to that of another abrasive leader[27]:

As she became known to the world as the "Iron Lady," [Margaret] Thatcher grew more and more convinced of the rightness of her ideas and the necessity of her coercive methods. She could beat anyone into submission with the power of her rhetoric and conviction, and she only got better at it. Eventually, though, it was her undoing—she was ousted by her own cabinet.

Jacob's growth as a leader would require a complete 180 from how he is leading currently as well as help from a leadership coach. To care more for the feelings of those he leads than his own, to take the time to build relationships with his team — it sounds like Jacob has his work cut out for him if he is to become truly effective at leading.

Although I said I wanted to end with Jacob, I'd like to add one more example about authenticity:

Dan

Embracing vulnerability has not come naturally to me. I was often aggressive, extremely ambitious, and unemotional (due at least in part to the trauma experienced from going to combat). At a young age, I was driven by accomplishments, results, and success, not culture or connection. How fast could I climb the promotion ladder? I was far removed from vulnerability or authenticity and did not align it with strength and confidence. Thankfully, I've matured and my growth journey toward being more vulnerable today. I realized I needed to consciously choose to change and challenge myself to admit I was wrong openly. I allowed others to coach me and highly encouraged feedback and criticism (and even thrived on it). As I embraced vulnerability, exposing my weak spots and inadequacies, it helped me close my own authenticity gap. It opened new doors for more robust, more fruitful professional and personal relationships. And, the doors to others' quality worlds opened up as they let me in.

In My Own Life:

Why I Wear Cowboy Boots

As I was preparing to separate from the Army, I made a choice to work with a recruiting firm to help me start my corporate career. I didn't realize it at the time, but the firm I worked with was big on "fake it until you make it." We went through interview rehearsal after interview rehearsal, and I practiced canned answers that were not really who I was. On their recommendation, I bought a suit from Brooks Brothers, for all the right reasons and reasons people tell themselves today — "People won't take you seriously if you're not in a suit," or "You should always dress one level above the customer." But I soon realized that specific business persona wasn't me — going from a military uniform to a stuffy jacket, slacks, and a tie felt inauthentic. I felt like I was trying to portray myself as someone I was not. I felt like I was lying about who I was, and it created a lot of cognitive dissonance and stress within my authenticity gap.

Today, my identity is aligned with how I would like others to see me. I wear nice blue jeans, cowboy boots, and a sports coat because I don't like the stuffiness of a suit and tie — I will "dress up" if the situation dictates, but I will more than likely show up as who I am. Part of that sartorial choice pays respect to my dad, a blue-collar entrepreneur and small-business owner in the residential and commercial HVAC industry. He worked hard every day in jeans and boots, forged authentic relationships with his employees and customers, and was very successful.

But most of it is my decision to be genuine to myself or authentic as a human being. I pride myself on not being your typical consultant, stiff and steeped in consulting protocols. My practice is built on being authentic and comfortable with my clients, just as I want them to be authentic and comfortable with me. I seek to establish a partnership, working with my clients instead of on them.

My former business partner will be the first to admit that my wardrobe choice made her nervous. And to be honest, I wasn't entirely sure how CEOs would react to how I dressed. But what I learned was that most clients enjoyed my attire. The leaders I work with appreciate someone who shows up real, not one who is putting on airs because they're talking to the CEO. It immediately creates a sense of comfort and familiarity, that they don't have to be polished when speaking with me or more concerned with how something they said comes across than understanding new truths about themselves and their situation.

Of course, there are limits — I'm not attending a business meeting in a nightgown in the name of authenticity. Your attire also denotes respect (respect for yourself, respect for the client), and it's important that whatever your personal style is, it's broad enough to accommodate professionalism. But I believe my blue jeans, boots, and sports coat signify that I'm here to help — authentically.

This story is concluded in the Afterword.

Cynthia, Anne, and Jacob each chose authenticity over leadership, instead of authentic leadership. In truth, all three of them are letting their desire to be authentic hold them back from growing as leaders. This paradox can be described this way[27]:

Countless books and advisers tell you to start your leadership journey with a clear sense of who you are. But that can be a recipe for staying stuck in the past. Your leadership identity can and should change each time you move on to bigger and better things.

Leading with authenticity is a balancing act, sharing yourself in a way that builds your relationship with your team instead of interfering with it. It requires knowing yourself and knowing your team[39]:

Authenticity ... is about giving a message about your true self — one you must continually shape and deliver by thoughtfully choosing your words and behaviors to suit the people you interact with and the specific purpose at hand.

IN MY OWN LIFE:

LIKE, COMMENT, SHARE

When we talk about the authenticity gap in a professional setting, it's often couched in the context of our work-selves — putting forth an image of a competent, confident business leader, regardless of our true feelings. But humans are multifaceted, even in who we appear to be in the office, and there are multiple ways to be authentic, or inauthentic, as a leader. I think this post from LinkedIn accurately relays the emotional and cognitive toll people go through to maintain the authenticity gap — bravo to this person who decided it was time to close it.

Last week, I was let go. Fired. Terminated. No company-wide layoffs. Just me.

Too often I find myself painting a veneer of success to the outside world. My social media posts have nothing but smiling participants. My LinkedIn updates (up until now) contain only career highlights. But the reality is I have experienced just as many (if not more) valleys than peaks on this journey through life.

I'm not sharing this as a preview of some future commencement speech where I affirm that it was all for the best, because I honestly don't know that to be true. Nor am I asking for any sympathy. I've been blessed far more than I deserve.

> I am sharing this because I am tired of maintaining that veneer.
> I'm not going to lie, this situation is incredibly difficult. I have
> no idea what I will do next. And I will fail at some point again
> in the future. But if admitting that publicly brings comfort to
> just one other person facing similar thoughts/feelings, then it
> was worth it.

Social media enables the authenticity gap to grow exponentially
since you can take as many perfect pictures as you want until just
the right one is viewed, edited, and shared. Then you wait for
everyone you know to like, comment, and share. And if no one
does, then you begin to wonder what's wrong with you. If you
were authentic from the start, you'd never have to question if you
were good enough, you'd know.

What Authentic Leadership Isn't

We spent a lot of time talking about what authentic leadership
is. Before wrapping up this section, let's take a moment looking at
what it's not.

- *Authentic leadership is not self-indulgent.* Remember
  Cynthia, who confided in her reports that she essentially
  was not ready for the mantle of leadership? Many of the
  leaders I've worked with don't struggle with being authentic
  as much as *leading authentically.* They forget their role and
  responsibilities as a leader and overshare. (After all, some
  things in Johari's "Not Known to Others" quadrant — like
  a leader's predilection for sleeping in the nude — should
  remain only Not Known to Others.) They confide when
  they shouldn't, maybe as a release from the pressures of
  leadership, maybe because they blur the line between
  "direct report" and "friend." As Adam Grant reminded us to
  kick off this chapter, authentic leadership still puts the needs
  of the organization and team ahead of your own, and that
  means *leading.*

This is especially the case in times of crisis. As we've seen during the COVID pandemic and will explore in the next chapter on humility, leadership counts the most in unexpected times of turbulence and uncertainty. In these moments, do you want your CEO to authentically share with everyone that they are frozen with fear and doubt, are self-medicating, or have trouble even getting up to face the team? Or would you prefer a CEO who keeps their fears and doubts to themselves around the team, who works on those fears and doubts *offline* with trusted advisors, and who calmly, steadily makes the best decisions they could with the information at hand, and with their fears and doubts in a private background?

- ***Authentic leadership is not an excuse for poor behavior.*** What happens when the overt expression of one's "true self" leads to some very toxic dynamics? Like was suggested above with Jacob, a leader who is quick to anger — and expresses such emotion "authentically" and openly — will likely serve to erode the psychological safety of their team. Removing filters and saying you're "just being yourself" at the expense of others isn't being authentic — it's being immature, disrespectful, and unprofessional. When a leader says this, they are now just using it to excuse their own poor behavior.

- ***Authentic leadership doesn't excuse living outside your values.*** These days, it's easy to confuse authenticity with nobility or morality. How many teenage pop stars seem to sing authentically about relationship issues they've never experienced? How many television commercials use authenticity to play on your feelings to make a sale? Closer to my experiences as a soldier, how many of history's villains like Hitler, Osama Bin Laden, or Saddam Hussein had convinced thousands of followers to do abhorrent things through authentic leadership? If you're an aspiring leader, it's important to lead with authenticity, but also to lead responsibly aligned with your values and pursue ethical goals.

- ***Authentic leadership isn't faking until you make it.*** Like living outside of your values, faking it is just deception of yourself and others. Elizabeth Holmes (whom we'll discuss in Chapter 5, **Choosing to be Vulnerable**) and her company Theranos are an example of complete and total deception. She faked until she made it, but in the end it was uncovered she wasn't authentic at all. Faking it simply isn't worth it.

Examine your leadership style. Do you lead with authenticity? Do you practice measured authenticity and adapt it to suit different contexts? Appendix 3 encourages you to explore methods to enhance your leadership authenticity and identify your authenticity gaps.

A tool that many companies use to shrink the authenticity gap — and one I strongly endorse and recommend during my coaching sessions — is a 360-degree assessment. A 360-degree assessment is a survey conducted among the people you interact with — peers, direct reports, and individuals throughout the management hierarchy, including those outside your immediate team. This survey gathers their insights on your effectiveness, strengths, and areas for improvement.

When combined with development plans to change specific behaviors, this feedback can be a practical way to demonstrate leadership growth through your actions. Finding a high-quality 360-degree assessment can be challenging, so we often use the Hogan 360. However, regardless of the tool you select, it's crucial to ensure that your coach or HR representative provides guidance or training to the respondents on how to give constructive feedback. Too often, if respondents are not informed on how to provide useful input, the feedback can quickly become useless.

AUTHOR'S REFLECTION:

RESPONDING TO THE AUTHENTIC LEADERSHIP DEBATE

In recent years, several respected scholars and practitioners have challenged the idea that "authentic leadership" is as effective or meaningful as once believed. Tomas Chamorro-Premuzic (*There Is Nothing Authentic About Authentic Leadership*, 2025[118]), Jeffrey Pfeffer (*Leadership BS*, 2015[119]), and Dennis Tourish *(The Inauthenticity of Authentic Leadership Theory*, 2023[120]) each argue that the theory has drifted into idealism, flawed research, and moral simplification.

Their critiques share a central concern: that being "true to oneself" often conflicts with the realities of leading others. They remind us that leadership is not a moral seminar but a disciplined practice that requires adaptability, self-control, and strategic impression management.

Chamorro-Premuzic calls authenticity a "feel-good theory" that adds little predictive power beyond transformational leadership. He points out that followers' perceptions—the so-called *halo effect*— often determine whether a leader seems authentic, regardless of the leader's actual intent or self-awareness. In his view, effective leaders are not radically transparent but rather skilled "method actors" who flex their behavior to meet the needs of others.

Tourish takes the critique further, arguing that much of Authentic Leadership Theory (ALT) rests on circular logic, idealized portrayals of leaders, and untested assumptions that "authentic" automatically means "good." He asks the provocative question: *What if a leader's true self is not inherently virtuous?* His point is not cynicism, but realism—human beings are complex, and authenticity must account for that complexity.

These critiques raise valid warnings: ***authenticity without discernment becomes self-indulgence.***

Unfiltered honesty can erode trust, and "bringing your whole self to work," including your frustrations and insecurities, can burden rather than inspire those you lead.

Where Leadership Begins Differs

In *Where Leadership Begins*, authenticity is not about radical transparency or self-expression. It's a **conscious choice** grounded in **Choice Theory**: the decision to align one's behavior with values in ways that strengthen relationships and build trust.

Authentic leadership, as I describe it, is not passive self-disclosure. It is active self-regulation.

It is about:

- Choosing to be aware of how others experience you.

- Choosing to act consistently with your values even when it's uncomfortable.

- Choosing to build trust through transparency that serves others, not yourself.

- Choosing to be courageous enough to adapt without losing your moral center.

If Chamorro-Premuzic is correct that great leaders are skilled impression managers, then *Choice Theory* explains *why* that matters: effective leaders consciously choose to manage impressions that preserve integrity and connection. They are not faking it. They are focusing it. They are choosing it.

Tourish's critique also reinforces why this approach matters. *Where Leadership Begins* acknowledges that leaders are not flawless moral actors. Authenticity, in this model, is not about uncovering a perfect inner self but about exercising moral agency, choosing which parts of ourselves we bring forward to serve others well.

Measured Authenticity: The Balance Point

Leadership is a delicate dance between sincerity and strategy. Too little authenticity breeds distrust, while too much can lead to self-indulgence or loss of credibility. Measured authenticity, or what I term functional authenticity, is the equilibrium where self-awareness, humility, and courage converge.

For example:

- **Too Little Authenticity** → Inconsistency, distrust

- **Too Much Authenticity** → Oversharing, unfiltered emotion

- **Functional Authenticity** → Strategic congruence between values and context.

Leaders who practice measured authenticity don't hide behind façades, but they also don't treat vulnerability as confession. They curate their openness and image for the benefit of others. They choose transparency that strengthens confidence, not undermines it. It is transparency with purpose.

Why Authentic Leadership Still Matters

Tourish is right to challenge the mythology surrounding authentic leadership, but his critique underscores the need for something deeper, not the need to abandon the concept entirely. When grounded in emotional intelligence, ethical clarity, and humility, authenticity remains a powerful force for trust, engagement, and psychological safety. These are not "soft" outcomes; they are the foundations of performance, retention, and innovation.

The critics are right to warn against naïve authenticity, but wrong to dismiss it altogether.

Leadership without authenticity becomes manipulation; authenticity without discernment becomes chaos.

Real leadership is the deliberate balance between the two.

Authentic leadership still matters, especially when it begins with choice.

CHAPTER ❹

CHOOSING TO BE HUMBLE

*"Humility is not thinking less of yourself
but thinking of yourself less."*
— C. S. Lewis

Why Do You Want To Be a Leader?

Have you ever stopped to consider *why* you want to be a leader? Take a moment to practice your skills of self-awareness and authenticity, and honestly explore why being a leader is essential to you.

I suspect if you've gotten this far in the book, you probably know that answers like "for a pay increase," "to earn the respect of my peers," or especially, "I'm gifted at telling people what to do," are likely not why your organization is turning toward you for leadership. Yet even people currently in leadership roles struggle with this question. For many, the answer is "I had nowhere else to go in my career," "An opening was available, and I had the most experience," or "I wanted to make my mark on the organization." This way of thinking has been explained this way[40]:

Much too often, people become leaders because doing so was merely the next logical step in their careers. They know what they want to *get* from the position (e.g., a new challenge, more prestige, better pay) but many have a tenuous grasp on what they hope to *give*. **Sure, they've got a reason to lead but they are vague about their purpose.**

For many aspiring leaders, the goal is to get noticed and demonstrate to others in the organization that they have the self-confidence, decisiveness, vision, and desire to lead — more so than any other candidate under consideration. It's a competition they want to win, and the leadership position is the prize. In and of themselves, these traits are not bad things in a leader, but they can have a dark side too. Too much charisma, for example, is linked to narcissism and can come with disastrous side effects.[41]

It's interesting to consider that these would-be leaders need to choose to be *humble*, of all things. That flies in the face of everything people have come to expect from leaders. It's not glamourous. Yet humility — sincere humility — is often the very thing that separates managers from true leaders and can ensure results, productivity, and effectiveness across and throughout an organization. Simply put, you can't be an effective leader without it.

What Is Humility?

The idea of a "humble leader" is foreign to many executives. After all, the picture we have of a leader is like our four-star general or the basketball coach from the Introduction — someone who knows all the answers, who has the charisma, the vision, and strategic ability to bring about an important victory.

First, let's step back and look at what it means to be humble. Here is one common misunderstanding of humility[42]:

In a 2016 College of Charleston survey, 56% of 5th and 6th graders said that the humble are embarrassed, sad, lonely, or shy. When adults are asked to recount an experience of humility, they often tell a story about a time when they were publicly humiliated.

Even our friend Aristotle defined humility as inordinate self-deprecation or exaggerated meekness. He considered humility more of a vice instead of a virtue.

Perhaps people conflate "humble" and "humbled," or associate the word "humble" with ordinariness, 'meekness or deference' [112] — a quality we don't typically associate with leaders we're supposed to look up to. In ancient times, many understood humility as lowliness, being close to the ground; why would a person stoop to be lower, bringing them closer to the dirt?[43]

In the context of leadership, though, humility takes on a different meaning. It refers to someone willing to put the interests of the team or organization ahead of themselves. Someone who understands that he or she doesn't have all the answers, who is willing to listen to and heed the advice of the experts on the team. It is humbleness that enables leaders to foster a high degree of openness, trust, and collaboration.

The humble leader understands their limitations and knows it's not about how brilliant they are.[44] According to recent research[42]:

True humility ... is when someone has an accurate assessment of both his strengths and weaknesses, and he sees all this in the context of the larger whole. He's part of something greater than he. He knows he isn't the center of the universe. And he's both grounded and liberated by this knowledge. Recognizing his abilities, he asks how he can contribute. Recognizing his flaws, he asks how he can grow.

Here's another important characterization[45]:

Humility is freedom from pride and arrogance: the state of low self-preoccupation. Humility is an understanding that every human is equally valuable; a recognition that you [as a leader] are worth no more or less than anyone else.

Wait — weaknesses? Flaws? Worth only as much as everyone else?

All of us are human — even leaders. And as humans, we have flaws and we make mistakes. How you acknowledge and address your mistakes speaks volumes about what kind of leader you are.

- An arrogant leader will deny those flaws to protect his or her ego. Arrogant leaders will insist they have all the answers, issues orders, and failure is blamed on others, even members of their team. After all, they reason, you're either a leader or a follower, and if you're a follower, by definition, you're looking to the leader for the answers. These people are often drawn to leadership because of the power the role gives them and the illusion they have influence.[44]

- A humble leader, one who is self-aware, authentic, and open to feedback, sees setbacks as opportunities for growth and has the courage, trust, and self-confidence to rely on his or her team. Humble leaders are focused on two things: the goals of the organization and the role their team plays in attaining them.

Note that a humble leader should not be confused with a passive one. And humility should not be conflated with false modesty, which is simply another form of pride. Humble leaders can passionately advocate for their teams and insist on accountability — of themselves, their teams, and their colleagues. They are also better risk-takers because they are more likely to be aware of their own shortcomings, have built up their team's capabilities, and earned the trust of their peers, and thus can rely on them for any needed advice. You can be certain if a humble leader is taking a risk, it's not for personal gain — it's because they think it will benefit the organization.

IN MY OWN LIFE:

THE HUMBLE PARROT

Anytime I think of the intersection of leadership and humility, I'm reminded of this joke. The keen-eyed reader likely sees a connection to choice theory too.

A young man named John received a parrot as a gift. The parrot had a bad attitude and an even worse vocabulary — every word out of its mouth was rude, obnoxious, and laced with profanity. John tried and tried to change the bird's attitude by consistently saying only polite words, playing soft music, and anything else he could think of to "clean up" the bird's vocabulary.

Finally, John was fed up, and he yelled at the parrot. The parrot yelled back. John shook the parrot, and the parrot got angrier and even ruder.

John, in desperation, threw up his hands, grabbed the bird and put him in the freezer. For a few minutes the parrot squawked and kicked and screamed. Then suddenly there was total quiet. Not a peep was heard for over a minute. Fearing that he'd hurt the parrot, John quickly opened the freezer door.

The parrot calmly stepped out onto John's outstretched arms and said, "I believe I may have offended you with my rude language and actions. I'm sincerely remorseful for my inappropriate transgressions, and I fully intend to do everything I can to correct my rude and unforgivable behavior." John was stunned at the change in the bird's attitude.

He was about to ask the parrot what had made such a dramatic change in his behavior, when the bird continued, "May I ask what the turkey did?"

You may now laugh, or at least smile a bit. I'd like to think William Glasser would have appreciated it, at least.

A humble leader is not a weak leader. Too often we associate humility with being weak — nothing could be further from the truth. Gandhi, whose autobiography is a journey of humbling self-dissection, once famously said, "I claim to be a simple individual liable to err like any other fellow mortal. I own, however, that I have humility enough to confess my errors and to retrace my steps."

Truly humble leaders are able to offer this kind of gift to us because they see and accept their own strengths and limitations without defensiveness or judgment — a core dimension of humility according to researchers from the University of California-Riverside, and one that cultivates a powerful compassion for humanity.[46]

While many leaders are coached to sound humble in front of a crowd, that's not the same as choosing to lead with humility. Let's explore the behaviors that define humble leadership.

Traits of the Humble Leader

With pride comes disgrace, but with humility comes wisdom.
— Proverbs

In sports, you often hear a manager described as "a player's coach," or a coach a player wants to play for. That degree of engagement and loyalty is typically the product of a relationship where the player knows the coach is personally invested in the player and team. More often than not, it's a product of humble leadership.

IN MY OWN LIFE:

ABRAHAM LINCOLN AND HUMILITY

When you think about politics these days, I'm willing to bet "humble" isn't the first word that jumps to mind. When I think about the presidents who served in my lifetime, I would say the two who in my opinion were the most humble were George W.

Bush and Jimmy Carter. (I'll quickly add that this isn't necessarily an endorsement of either man's politics — I bet I could find good and bad things to say about both politicians' policies.)

But you know what else George W. Bush and Jimmy Carter had in common? A rotten 34% approval rating when they left office, according to the American Presidency Project at the University of California — Santa Barbara.[47] If we excluded President Nixon (who resigned in disgrace in 1974), you'd have to go back to Harry S. Truman in 1952 to find a lower approval rating upon leaving office.

Needless to say, humility alone hasn't been a sure recipe for success in modern politics, at least not at the presidential level.

However, that wasn't always the case. I happened across a TED talk by Doris Kearns Goodwin, a presidential historian and author of *Team of Rivals: The Political Genius of Abraham Lincoln*. During her presentation, Goodwin said this about our 16th President[48]:

> "He possessed an uncanny ability to empathize with and think about other people's point of view. He repaired injured feelings that might have escalated into permanent hostility. He shared credit with ease. He assumed responsibility for the failure of his subordinates. He constantly acknowledged his errors and learned from his mistakes. He refused to be provoked by petty grievances. He never submitted to jealousy or brooded over perceived slights."

It was his humble spirit that equipped him to demonstrate each of the seven leadership strengths Goodwin listed in that description. While it might seem out of place in today's politics, Lincoln's genuine humility enabled him to be such a strong yet gentle 19th-century leader.

A far cry from the traditional view of what a leader is, the humble leader:

- **Listens before speaking.** Instead of instructing the team that "we're going to do it this way," a humble leader solicits the team's insight first. Perhaps they will verify and buy into the leader's experience — or perhaps they'll supply a different perspective, one that might prompt the leader to re-examine their own thinking.

- ***Never stops learning.*** Whether it is about themselves, their organization, their clients, their competitors, or their industry, there will always be something new to learn and grow from. As soon as a leader thinks they know everything and have nothing new to learn, they're well on their way to obsolescence.

- ***Looks to serve.*** While leaders are entrusted with power, it's not to enrich themselves — it's to build up others on their team and the organization.

- ***Accepts blame.*** The humble leader does not pass blame onto others but welcomes and accepts it, sees it as an opportunity to grow, and learns from it. The humble leader also does not shy away from holding others accountable when and where needed.

- ***Shares the credit.*** The humble leader is not threatened by others or does not feel the need to prove themselves over and over. They delegate responsibility and reward others with credit, praise, and accountability. They can also accept credit with thanks.

- ***Does not put too much stock in titles.*** A title does not change who a leader is fundamentally — their experiences, their values, their judgment. The titles of others in the organization might reflect valuable experiences, but they shouldn't discount the perspectives of on-the-ground team members who lack a title.

- ***Forgives and even forgets.*** Mistakes are to be addressed and learned from, without question. But a humble leader does not hold grudges or does not let others' past mistakes cloud their judgment.

- **Balances self-confidence.** A humble leader often demonstrates quiet confidence, assertiveness, and a clear vision for the organization, coupled with exceptional humility in motivating the team to improve performance. By recognizing their limitations, they direct their energy toward supporting the team rather than focusing on themselves. Because they know their boundaries, they are more likely to confidently delegate tasks effectively. This combination of self-confidence and humility is essential for effective leadership. [112]

- **Is ambitious about their work, team, or organization, but not themselves.** They recognize leadership is really a team sport. They're not afraid to try or even take risks, because they know the reasoning behind that behavior comes from what's best for their team and organization.

- **Is fiercely competitive.** Highly effective and humble leaders are fiercely competitive and ambitious about their work, team, or organization, but not themselves. They recognize leadership as a team sport. They're not afraid to try and take risks because they know the reasoning behind that behavior comes from what's best for their team and organization. They don't take themselves seriously. They take business success seriously. [113]

- **Leads in an open and public fashion for everyone to see.** Those who work with this kind of leader might say, "What you see is what you get" — and mean it as a compliment. This is the authentic leader from Chapter 3, where the inner circle supports the outer circle, and there is little to no authenticity gap.

- **Creates engagement.** A humble leader creates engagement by building trust with others through their actions. For instance, they listen to feedback without defensiveness, share credit for successes, take responsibility for failures, delegate properly, admit mistakes, and consistently prioritize the advancement of organizational goals over personal ones. Trustworthiness is the principal factor in employee engagement.[112]

- ***Builds psychological safety.*** A humble leader fosters psychological safety by modeling behaviors that encourage openness, learning, and mutual respect. The humble leader builds trust and acceptance, enabling team members to express themselves freely without fearing judgment or reprisal, fostering learning and growth.

Lastly, the true mark of humble leadership is that they develop other humble leaders from their team. Rather than feeling threatened by the success of those under them, they encourage the growth and success of the people they lead and encourage them to become leaders of their own.

Each of these behaviors has its own risks. If you admit to not having all the answers, you risk compromising your authority. If you promote others on your team over yourself, you risk missing out on the praise and attention of senior leaders or industry leaders. However, when humble leadership is balanced and demonstrated appropriately, the rewards of choosing to be humble far outweigh the risks.

The Benefits of Humble Leadership

"Humble leaders create engagement."
— Robert Hogan, PhD, founder and president of Hogan Assessments

Because humility focuses on the self and internal processes, it might seem that the benefits of choosing to be humble would be felt at the individual level. However, research has found that the effects can be felt throughout the organization when leaders practice humility. Notably, team and organization performance increases exponentially. Here are some benefits your organization can receive when leaders choose to be humble.

- **Productivity and innovation.** Is innovation important to you and your organization? One study of inclusive leadership reported[49] that "inclusion was linked both to employees' self-reported innovation and team citizenship — behaviors that can have a profound impact on overall team productivity and product innovation." They also identified humility as one of four key leadership behaviors linked to inclusion, and that "humility ... can go a long way in making leaders more inclusive and effective." An arrogant leader who dictates to others how operations are to be run discourages engagement and creativity. In contrast, humble leaders who put the team over themselves are more likely to be rewarded with greater team commitment and outside-the-box thinking.

- **Employee growth and development.** Research suggests[50] that "leaders who want to grow signal to followers that learning, growth, mistakes, uncertainty, and false starts are normal and expected in the workplace, and this produces followers and entire organizations that constantly keep growing and improving." The study's authors found that these findings applied to all kinds of organizations, "military, manufacturing, health care, financial services, retailing and religious." Humble leaders are naturally inclined to building up their employees and helping them grow. This often results in organizations that are more capable and have better resiliency.

- **Better decision-making.** Would your organization benefit from a leader who stays cool under fire? That trait could be developed through humility[51]: "Humble leaders know how to keep things in perspective. ... They can take a step back from a problem to look at the bigger picture, to look back and around for a better perspective, and to see things from another's viewpoint." Humble leaders understand that the world around them constantly changes, and that solutions that worked yesterday might not still work today.

Rather than committing to a preconceived course of action, they're more likely to be open to new opportunities and possibilities.

- ***Greater employee satisfaction and performance.*** One study[42] found that "humble leaders prioritize the organization's success ahead of their own. ... They hired more diverse management teams, and they give staff the ability to lead and innovate. Humble leaders have less employee turnover, higher employee satisfaction, and they improve the company's overall performance." These insights echo Glasser's thoughts on the quality world: Humble leaders are better able to build relationships and trust and operate within each team member's quality world.

- ***More accurate industry assessments.*** Intellectual humility can also make you less susceptible to the scourge of modern times — "fake news." Research found[52] that "low intellectual humility is ... associated with the tendency to be threatened by what one doesn't know ... and with the motive to defend one's ego in the face of ignorance, errors, disagreements, and other signs of one's intellectual shortcomings." In other words, when you remain open to the idea that you don't necessarily have all the answers, you're more likely to consider new ways of thinking and less likely to "double down" on a wrong solution to save face.

- ***Increased collaboration and effectiveness.*** One study found[53] that humble leaders enhance team collaboration, information sharing, and joint decision-making. The research examined 105 small to medium-sized companies and discovered that humility and leadership had profoundly positive effects on performance and also showed increased team effectiveness when humility and leadership existed side by side.

Not surprisingly, especially in our every-changing environment, successful companies today and in the future will be the companies flooded with leaders that actively practice humility, admit their mistakes, listen to innovative and new ideas, and create a culture and environment abundant with opportunities for employees to help and be part of the solution.[54]

In My Own Life:

Humility Amid a Pandemic, Featuring Al Haig

The COVID-19 global pandemic has provided an incredible platform for leaders to exercise humility. The pandemic's uncertainty left business leaders looking for answers they did not have and grappled with supporting their communities, maintaining operations, and keeping people employed. Amid this uncertainty, the choice to be humble proved challenging for many leaders, as their hero-like self-image and ego drifted away just as fast as a pallet of toilet paper at Costco. Leaders were forced to reckon with themselves and level with their direct reports. The leaders who chose to embrace humility, showing compassion, care, and some level of personal struggle appeared to be more authentic, honest, and genuine. Humble leaders helped their employees face the reality of the situation by letting them know they cared and understood what they were going through, by demonstrating humility and measured authenticity (Free hand sanitizer, respecting staff by wearing a mask, simplified menus, and encouraging big tips for the brave employees).

One study argued[55] that to lead through this era of exponential change, leaders have to embrace humility, authenticity, and openness. When the world is rapidly changing and accelerating changes all around us, as the COVID-19 pandemic did, leaders who choose to be humble, authentic, and open instill trust and psychological safety.

Not only have I seen this bear out in the organizations I'm a part of (my church, my practice, my baseball team, my kids' school), but, like many of you, I've experienced it myself. I've asked some of the very same questions you might have asked yourself:

- How can I pursue what's important to me, including my livelihood, when everything suddenly (and unpreparedly) goes virtual?

- How can I balance my personal safety with liberty? When does cautious become too cautious?

- How do I maintain important personal relationships when we can't sit in the same room?

- How do the organizations I'm involved with progress when we can't even meet as an organization?

And, importantly for this conversation:

- Are the leaders I'm entrusting my safety to making decisions with my best interests in mind?

If you're a leader, these are the questions your reports and peers are struggling with, and turning to you for the answer. How can you respond confidently and definitively when the world around you is changing so rapidly?

The answer is, of course, you can't. Which means you have a new question to wrestle with:

- How can I lead with confidence when the answers keep changing — when the answers aren't even knowable?

You have two choices. On the one hand, you can fake it: You can answer definitively and confidently with a best guess and fingers crossed and hope for the best. The biggest problem (of many) with this approach is that, chances are, your team won't believe you. It reminds me of the assassination attempt of President Reagan in

1981, when Secretary of State Al Haig announced to the press he was "in charge" while the President was in surgery. G. Philip Hughes, the Vice President's Deputy Foreign Policy Advisor, described the situation this way[56]:

> When the assassination attempt on President Reagan occurred,... Al Haig came to the White House and he convened a meeting of the NSC to go over the situation with Reagan's advisors. There was of course great public anxiety, and someone had to go up and make a press statement.
>
> Either Haig nominated himself or someone nominated him but in any event he walked into the press room breathless. I remember watching this on TV from my office. He walked into the press room breathless. He looked perfectly flushed and frazzled....
>
> The Vice President had been notified and he was flying back from Texas and in the meantime Al Haig was in control at the White House. A particularly infelicitous choice of words which, I think, already in the minds of many Reagan supporters and staff, for Al Haig to come up and say that "I, Al Haig, am in control here at the White House," just convinced many people that, first of all he was intemperate and injudicious and not suited for the role, and further that he had vast ambitions of power in the administration which were not in keeping with the way that Reagan cabinet secretaries were expected to behave.

So frankly then there were a whole bunch of battles after that and Mr. Haig passed from the scene.

✶✶✶✶

Don't misunderstand — there is a need for leadership amid chaos, and Haig's instinct to reassure the country was correct. But whether it's an assassination attempt or a global pandemic, a show that you're on top of the situation when you clearly are not only undercuts your position of leadership.

The other choice, of course, is to answer with humility: You can admit to your team that there is no playbook for a once-in-a-century crisis, and while you don't have all the answers yet, you will be as open as you can be with the information you have. One study identified three best practices for leaders to communicate effectively during a pandemic and any crisis[57]:

- First, leaders should be open about what they know and what they don't know.

- Second, leaders must find the right tone and the right message.

- And third, when appropriate, leaders should take responsibility for their actions or failure to act.

This approach not only allows you to demonstrate flexibility and change according to what your organization's circumstances require,[55] but it's reassuring. Your team and colleagues know you're being candid and honest with them, and in a time of chaos, candor and honesty are a real show of trust and leadership.

The global pandemic has placed a hefty dose of humility in leaders' arms, especially those leaders with egos that remain unchecked. This is not to suggest that leaders should not be confident, because they should be. Confidence and ego are related insofar as when leaders become overly confident, they develop blind spots which is detrimental to the organization and employees. Humility is the antidote to overconfidence by staying aware, remaining alert, and being agile. Leaders should challenge their standard approach to decision-making and actively seek out other opinions, embrace listening, and admit when "they never thought of that," and ask others to collectively contribute to developing a solution.

We've seen how a humble leader behaves and how that behavior benefits an organization. Now let's look at some examples of how the humble leader acts, including a real-world example that shows the courage humble leadership can require.

Glasser and the Humble Leader

Leaders will likely find it difficult to establish quality-world connections with members of his or her team without this kind of humility. A leader who claims to have all the answers is likely to go straight to control theory ("I'm the leader, just do as I say."), while one who is looking to forge relationships with team members and elevate the team is likely to embrace choice theory. Consider this study's conclusions[58]:

A type-A, action-oriented, high-achiever may shudder at the terms "servant leader" or "humble leader," but studies show the power and influence these styles have on an organization. Humility is about honesty; it helps cut through the ego to overcome conflicts and create harmonious situations.

"Harmonious situations" are at the core of choice theory, especially in the workplace. In *The Language of Choice Theory,* Glasser and Glasser[3] offer an example of arrogant versus humble leadership, as seen in a vignette of an employee whose new boss is significantly younger than he is:

External Control

I know I'm twenty years younger than you. And I know I've only been here for three years and you've been here for thirty. But I'm your boss and I expect you to treat me as if I am. I want you at all the meetings just like everyone else. And on time.

Choice Theory Alternative

This is a tough situation. I'm your boss, and I'm younger than your oldest son. Computers have changed everything. You know that as well as I do. But there's only so much computers can do. They know a billion things, but they have no wisdom or experience. You've got both. You can help me if you want to. I'll listen to you.

This scenario involves many issues of leadership, but I especially want to look at the end:

They know a billion things, but they have no wisdom or experience. You've got both. You can help me if you want to. I'll listen to you.

This leader is acknowledging not only the strengths of the employee, but also his or her own limitations. This is the humble leader in action: By establishing a relationship with the employee rather than demanding compliance, the humble leader is far more likely to retain a committed and valuable resource.

Humility is a fundamental attitude; it is the opposite of arrogance. Arrogant people assume they are entitled to respect, status, and recognition. Humble people, alternatively, understand that they must earn respect, status, and recognition — in every interaction, every day.[45]

In My Own Life:

Food for Thought

If I asked you to name some of the most prominent leaders in today's society, what would you say? These days, our highest-profile leaders probably come from the business world, like Jeff Bezos or Mark Zuckerberg — entrepreneurs whose technological and financial successes have made them household names. But as you read accounts of Bezos taking trips to space and Zuckerberg recounting the animals he's killed by hand, it's worth asking: Are these titans of industry actually leaders?

Fortunately, not every successful entrepreneur today is this ... flamboyant. Let me share the stories of two of my favorite leaders in the business world — in this case, successful fast food executives who made a name for themselves by leading with humility and compassion.

Truett Cathy, Founder, Chick-Fil-A

Truett Cathy stood apart in today's world as someone who truly lived his faith and cared about the world. There are many stories about his humble beginnings, his commitment to his faith and the ways he gives back to his customers, employees, and community. One that particularly resonates with me was his choice to close his restaurant every Sunday, in keeping with his Christian faith[59]:

The practice of closing on Sundays has kept Chick-fil-A out of some lucrative venues, like sporting arenas and malls that require tenants to be open seven days a week. Yet in a May 11, 2007, interview in the *Atlanta Business Journal*, Truett stated that closing on Sundays is one of the best business decisions he ever made. "It's very important that we are consistent in our convictions. We dare not vary from it," he remarked. "I think people respect you for that and eat more often with you."

In 2014, *Time* published a remembrance commemorating Truett's passing, written by Rick Warren, pastor of Saddleback Church and best-selling author of *The Purpose Driven Life*. In it, he wrote[60]:

Truett was a man truly who lived his faith, welcoming the homeless into his own home, improving the lives of thousands of disadvantaged kids, and giving them help and hope. Even after becoming a billionaire CEO, Truett continued to teach his weekly Sunday School class for 50 years. One of the five books he wrote summed up his attitude toward helping young boys in trouble: *It's Better To Build Boys Than Mend Men*.

Truett Cathy's life is a good reminder, especially now, that being a billionaire business leader does not mean forsaking values of humility and service.

Cheryl Bachelder, CEO, Popeyes Louisiana Kitchen

When Cheryl Bachelder took over Popeyes Louisiana Kitchen as CEO in 2007, the fast food restaurant had already fallen on hard times. Its stock price had sunk to just $13 a share — barely a third of what it had been five years earlier. You might expect a restaurant in such dire straits to turn to a proven industry leader to help turn around their fortunes — not someone who was just fired from a rival chicken chain[61]:

My humbling experience was leading KFC and getting fired. I wasn't achieving results, and you have to have a strong strategic plan to serve the people well. I had the right style but not the right substance, and I wasn't successful. It was unsettling. It forced a lot of reflection. But I came out a better leader.

And did she ever. Bachelder brought a culture of servant leadership to Popeyes, and over her 10-year tenure as CEO the restaurant's turnaround was nothing short of remarkable[62]:

- More than $1 billion in U.S. sales

- The number one franchise partner with 95% satisfaction levels

- Growth of both restaurant revenues (by 45%) and bottom-line profits (by more than 100%)

- A stock price that had risen to $79

But what most impresses me about Bachelder is how she did it. In an essay on humility and confidence, she recounted a presentation from three regional leaders addressing the Popeyes board. The presenters were warm and confident and shared both successes and challenges. But what stayed with her was something different entirely[63]:

Perhaps it was what was missing from their presentations, that made them most impressive. Among the three leaders, there was none of the following:

1. Oneupmanship: the need to evidence that they were better than their colleagues

2. Bravado: excessive descriptions of their personal role in the circumstances

3. Ego: need to be recognized and celebrated, apart from the team

That's something I think is missing from so many leaders today — the humility and desire to serve. I realize that maybe that makes me sound old-fashioned, but I don't think these things are a forgotten relic from a Truett Cathy and Cheryl Bachelder, they prove it.

A Living Example of Humble Leadership

Being a humble leader might sound like it's easy. Rest assured, it's not. Consider the following example from a Milwaukee manufacturing company[64]:

At Rockwell Automation, a leading provider of manufacturing automation, control, and information solutions, practicing humility in these ways has been essential to promoting an inclusive culture — a culture Rockwell's leaders see as critical to leveraging the diversity of its global workforce.

One of the key strategies they've adopted to model this leadership style is the fishbowl — a method for facilitating dialogue. At a typical fishbowl gathering, a small group of employees and leaders sit in a circle at the center of the room, while a larger group of employees are seated around the perimeter. Employees are encouraged to engage with each other and leaders on *any* topic and are invited into the innermost circle. In these unscripted conversations, held throughout the year in a variety of venues, leaders routinely demonstrate humility — by admitting to employees that they don't have all the answers and by sharing their own personal journeys of growth and development.

At one fishbowl session, shortly after the company introduced same-sex partner benefits in 2007, a devoutly religious employee expressed concerns about the new benefits policy — in front of hundreds of other employees. Rather than going on the defensive, a senior leader skillfully engaged that employee in dialogue, asking him questions and probing to understand his perspectives. By responding in this way, the leader validated the perspectives of that employee and others who shared his views. Other leaders shared their own dilemmas and approaches to holding firm to their own religious beliefs yet embracing the company's values of treating *all* employees fairly. Dialogues such as these have made a palpable difference at Rockwell Automation. Employees have higher confidence in their leaders, are more engaged, and feel more included — despite their differences.

IN MY OWN LIFE:

HUMILITY IN EVERYDAY LIFE

Rockwell is not the only example of humility I've encountered in Milwaukee.

I first visited the city in February of 2007 in the middle of a blizzard. Interestingly, I fell in love with Milwaukee and the people that embodied the area during that visit. One of my favorite stories to share is when I met the then-Archbishop (now Cardinal) Timothy Dolan of the Archdiocese of Milwaukee.

✷ ✷ ✷ ✷

It was March 2007 and my first day working in Milwaukee. At the time, I was living in the Hilton Milwaukee City Center until my family could move here and into temporary corporate housing. It was a great day — it was cold and sunny, and it smelled like fresh manufacturing across downtown. I put on my business attire, headed to my car, and drove the few minutes to the off-main-campus office where I would call my work home for many months. I don't remember all the details of my first day, but I know I was excited to begin my first post-military corporate job. I met lots of new people that I ended up working with in some fashion and took tours of the facilities. As most onboarding activities are filled with meetings, mine was no different.

After completing my first day of the rest of my career, I was smiling from ear to ear, ecstatic about working for this storied company. I headed back to my car for my short drive back to my hotel room.

Exhausted from the day and still unfamiliar with the area, I decided to take up dinner at the nearby ChopHouse.

The Milwaukee ChopHouse is a great fine dining restaurant, and I decided to celebrate my first day with a nice prime rib and all the fixings. When I entered the restaurant, it was close to being empty, with only three or four other groups of people having dinner. The server led me at my table, and I sat facing the entrance where I could see who was coming and going. Toward the end of my meal, I noticed two men enter the restaurant — an older gentleman in a business suit and a tall, bigger man in a black clergyman suit and collar.

After a brief conversation, the server led them to their seats. Being a Catholic myself, I was intrigued by the clergyman — you don't see priests out in the wild too often. I watched them walk from the entrance to a booth all the way on the other side of the restaurant. After a brief chat with the server, though, they seemed unhappy with the seating arrangement, and the server sat them at a table right next to mine.

As the man in the business suit sat down, the clergyman observed me sitting by myself and struck up a conversation with me. "Hey, how's the food? What are you doing here?" he asked. I sort of sheepishly said the food was good and that I had just moved here after leaving the military, and today was my first day. If you know Cardinal Dolan, you know he is an imposing figure, loud and gregarious, so this next part won't surprise you.

After I shared my brief story, he loudly proclaimed, "Well, welcome! You are going to love it here!" He shook my hand and patted me on the back as he was sitting down. For the next few minutes, he proceeded to talk with me about the area and the places I should visit. After about 20 minutes, our conversation began to wrap up, and he asked if I happened to be Catholic. I responded, "Actually I am a Catholic." "I like you even better now," he said. "Hey, here's my card — I am the Milwaukee Archbishop, and if you need anything, email me and I'll let you know my thoughts."

I was flabbergasted. This man — the highest-ranking Catholic in the area and a local icon — put no stock in his title, and looking to continue to serve gave me his card and told me to email him. Wow.

There are a couple of things that I happen to believe in as a result of this experience:

First, I believe God intervened in my life. I had a choice, and I chose to include him in my quality world. Here is an excerpt from an email I sent him:

> When I first knew that I was going to be interviewing for a job in Milwaukee I conducted extensive research online to learn more about the city, culture and area. One fact that I discovered that drew me in was that Milwaukee is 58% Catholic. For me I was already sold. Then I visited and saw the culture, the cathedrals, Marquette University, and then meeting you last night. You and the gentleman could have sat in the booth on the other side of the restaurant, but I truly believe that God put us together last night. I believe there was a true meaning behind last night and was not a coincidence. The Lord is shining His light on my path towards Him, and I shall come to Milwaukee and expand my faith here with my family and to others.

Second, I believe the humble example he demonstrated not only that night, but in the relationship we subsequently developed over the years prior to his elevation to Cardinal and move to New York, is what makes for the great story here, right now. He could have walked into the restaurant wielding his position and asked for the best seat in the house or even a private room, but that was not who he was. He also could have chosen to not talk to me. He was at the ChopHouse with a guest, but he chose to humbly give some of his precious time. And he didn't tell me who he was until he needed to — it wasn't important because he put me first.

We chose to put each other in our quality worlds and developed a long relationship that I look upon still today and cherish as a great example of true humility.

Think of the people you know currently in leadership roles. How many do you know would feel comfortable in a fishbowl like this?

- Inviting a public discussion of topics for which they didn't have pre-vetted talking points

- Candidly sharing their closely held opinions and experiences with a large group

- Embracing uncertainty

- Listening to and seeing multiple perspectives of an issue *yet* holding firm on the company policy — in a way that doesn't dismiss those who disagree

This is not a task for the narcissist, prideful, or arrogant leader, one who would likely tell an employee who disagrees with policy "well, that's just the way it is," or "if you don't like it you can just leave," or, even worse, redirecting the conversation to themselves and away from the issue and question at hand. By being open, honest, and humble, a leader strengthens engagement and becomes someone team members *want* to work with and for.

Humility Does Not Guarantee Success

"If you're not humble in this world, then
this world will throw humbleness upon you."
— Mike Tyson

One final note about humble leadership — as important as it is for an organization to develop humble leaders, we saw with Cynthia in the previous chapter on authenticity what happens when a leader substitutes humility for actual leadership. Your role as a leader still needs to be filled, and leaders need to be held accountable for not only their team's performance, but their own as well. One study explains[65] that in times when a leader is called for:

… members are likely to expect you to take charge and make important decisions. In these circumstances, showing weakness through humility can be counterproductive. This doesn't mean that you shouldn't display humility at all. You can still be open about your limitations and weaknesses, but it's better to do so while simultaneously demonstrating that you have the ability to overcome and learn from your shortcomings and lead your team to improve and grow. This allows you to harvest the advantage of displaying humility in encouraging creativity *and* show the confidence and power that matches your team's expectations.

IN MY OWN LIFE:

CHOOSING HUMILITY: AMY'S LEADERSHIP IN TRANSITION

Amy is a close friend of my family, and as I observed her situation, I was struck by an incredible story that exemplifies true humility in leadership. Amy faced a significant personal setback when she lost her position, yet she chose to serve others without resentment or ego. Rather than focusing on what she was losing, her attention was on what her team needed. Here is Amy's inspiring story of choosing humility.

✳ ✳ ✳ ✳

Amy sat quietly in her office, the email from leadership still open on her screen. The decision was final: her role had been eliminated as part of a middle-management reduction at one of the major health systems in the Milwaukee area. After years of dedication and countless hours supporting her team and driving performance, the news hit hard. She knew she had a choice—walk away immediately or stay for the next 30 days to ensure a smooth transition. The thought of leaving in such circumstances was daunting, but Amy's unwavering belief in the power of humility in leadership guided her decision.

Despite the disappointment, Amy consciously chose not to leave in frustration. Her deep care for the team she had nurtured and her commitment to their success made the thought of abandoning them without setting them up for success unbearable. This was her moment to embody humility—leading even when she was no longer required to. Her selfless decision to stay and serve her team despite her personal loss is truly inspiring.

Choosing to Stay Despite the Loss

Amy met with her team the day after receiving the news, knowing she had to approach the conversation carefully. She didn't want the uncertainty to breed fear or confusion among her staff.

"I wanted to share some news with all of you directly," she began, her voice steady. "Due to changes in the organization, my role is being eliminated. My last day will be in 30 days." She paused, allowing the information to settle before continuing, "But what's most important to me right now is ensuring this transition goes as smoothly as possible—for you and our new hires. I'll stay on during this time to support each of you, help with onboarding, and ensure our management processes are handed off effectively."

At first, the team sat in stunned silence. A few staff members offered words of support, but they were primarily worried about what would come next.

"Don't worry," Amy reassured them. "We're going to get through this together. I'm here to help you every step of the way."

Serving with Humility During Transition

Over the next several weeks, Amy threw herself into the transition work—not because she had to, but because she cared. Her goal wasn't to leave the organization on a good note for personal reputation; it was about her team and their success. Every task she completed was done with humility, knowing that the focus needed to be on the future, not what she had lost.

One of her priorities was onboarding the new hires she had recently recruited. Despite the emotional weight of leaving, she sat with each new employee individually to welcome them properly and walk them through the organization's processes. She wanted them to feel valued from day one, knowing their success would contribute to the team's stability.

"Even though I won't be here long-term, my goal is to ensure you have everything you need to succeed," Amy told one of the new hires during orientation. "Your success is what matters most to me right now."

Amy also mentored other team members who would be stepping up to take on additional responsibilities in her absence. She organized one-on-one coaching sessions, offering advice on everything from managing workloads to fostering team morale.

"When you're leading, it's not about doing everything yourself," she told a colleague during a coaching session. "It's about empowering others and knowing when to ask for help."

She even met with upper management to ensure all pending projects were documented correctly and transferred to the right individuals. She humbly acknowledged that her departure meant others would have to pick up the slack. "If there's anything I can do to make this handoff smoother, just let me know," she told the director overseeing the transition. "I want to leave things better than I found them."

Passing the Torch with Grace

On her final day, Amy gathered her team for one last meeting. There were no grand speeches or complaints about the situation—just a heartfelt expression of gratitude and encouragement.

"I want you to know how proud I am of everything we've accomplished together," she said, looking around the room at each person. "This team is strong, and I know you'll continue to thrive. Even though I won't be here, I'm confident you'll build on the foundation we've created."

She handed over her final project files, ensured everyone had the contact information they needed and gave everyone a few last words of encouragement. "You've got this," she said with a smile. "Just remember—lead humbly, listen to each other, and support your team."

Amy packed her things quietly when the meeting ended, slipping out of the office without fanfare. She didn't need recognition or applause. Her satisfaction came from knowing she had done everything possible to set her team up for success.

<u>The Legacy of Humility</u>

In the weeks following Amy's departure, the impact of her humility became evident. The team, buoyed by Amy's example, stayed on track and continued to thrive. The new hires felt welcomed and supported, and the manager who took on Amy's duties found they were more prepared than expected. The team's resilience in the face of change is a testament to Amy's leadership.

Upper management noted how smoothly the transition had gone. Even though Amy was no longer with the organization, her influence remained. The humility she demonstrated in those final 30 days— serving others without expectation of reward—left a lasting legacy within the team.

One of the employees who had taken over some of Amy's responsibilities reflected on the experience: "Amy could have left the day she got the news, but she didn't. She stayed for us. She showed us that leadership isn't just about holding a position—it's about showing up for others, even when it's hard."

<u>Lessons from Amy's Humility</u>

Amy's focus wasn't on what she was losing but on what her team needed. She demonstrated that authentic leadership is about lifting others up, even when you're on your way out. Amy's story teaches us that leadership is not about titles or recognition but about making a difference, even when no one is watching.

Amy modeled the essence of humility by staying on to support her team, ensuring new hires were onboarded properly, and passing on her responsibilities with care. She showed that leadership isn't about titles or recognition—it's about making a difference, even when no one is watching.

Her story reminds us that humility is a choice we make every day. It's the decision to put others first, to serve without expectation, and to leave things better than we found them.

Those who are more drawn to humble leadership would also do well to gain greater self-awareness and explore how their tendency toward humility could work against them. Research into humble leaders found[66] that, for all their positive leadership traits, humble leaders are less prone to rock the boat — even when rocking the boat is what's necessary to achieve positive change. They may also be perceived as cold or detached, and "can have a hard time rallying people through their own energy and enthusiasm."[51] When choosing to be humble, leaders need to be aware of how their humble behaviors affect those they interact with.

Taking a 3,000-foot-view: According to DDI,[67] roughly half of executives fail within their first two years on the job. The most common reason for their failure could be their inability to build and then maintain a team.[68] Abundant research suggests that humility predicts effective leadership, but emerging humble leaders must realize their effectiveness depends on their own understanding of interpersonal skills and their abilities when it comes to managing them for themselves and others.[69] It requires learning from self-awareness, through experiences, and from their own engagements and interactions with others.

The first step for a leader to develop humility is acknowledging that they are not humble. They need to understand that without it, they will fail. A leader who completely avoids learning from experience will likely gain a reputation for poor judgment and struggle to retain followers.[112]

Humble leaders have much to offer their direct reports, peers, and the broader organization they serve. So, how do you become a humble leader? Choose to be vulnerable (the next chapter) because vulnerability is the lifeblood of humility and can take many forms.

What about you? Are you a humble leader? Check out Appendix 4 for strategies for choosing and cultivating humility in your leadership approach.

CHAPTER ⑤

CHOOSING TO BE VULNERABLE

"In an organizational culture where respect and the dignity of individuals are held as the highest values, shame and blame don't work as management styles. There is no leading by fear."
— Brené Brown

"Ignore the haters. You're not the jackass whisperer."
— Scott Stratten

Previously in Chapter 3 we looked at authentic leadership and the authenticity gap:

141

We know that reducing the authenticity gap is essential to establishing honest, productive relationships with the members of your team — the kind of relationships that encourage others to be fully engaged in the mission of the organization and their role within it. But how do we get there? How do we narrow the gap, and go from there to here:

Your Behavior

Smaller
Authenticity
Gap

You

Your
Actions

Your
Speech

By embracing our own vulnerability.

This might be the most difficult choice effective leaders need to make. The idea so many of us are taught about leadership is that leaders need "to keep a distance and project a certain image. An image of confidence, competence and authority."[70] That to make the hard choices about the future of the organization, they can't have their thinking blurred by feelings. They need to be clear-headed and close-hearted, making decisions based entirely on logic and not muddied by personal relationships. To be vulnerable by definition seems to be an admission of weakness; to lead effectively, you need to build a wall of invulnerability.

It's very important to recognize that this wall of invulnerability many leaders choose to erect is (1) a conscious choice by the leader to insulate him or herself from others in the organization, and (2) almost certainly a bad and counterproductive idea.

Let's look more closely at what it means to be vulnerable and how vulnerability helps build relationships within an organization.

IN MY OWN LIFE:

BY ALL MEANS, LET'S WRITE A BOOK

The entire process of writing this book has been a significant exercise in vulnerability. To truly embrace vulnerability, you must learn to be comfortable with discomfort. Honestly, sharing my authentic self with you—perhaps a stranger reading this book—has made me uneasy. My doubts and insecurities are exposed to potential criticism and ridicule from my LinkedIn connections. Will the leadership guru I greatly respect dismiss my perspective as "psychobabble gobbledygook," or will he appreciate my effort to present these ideas in a consumable format?

At some point, we all must realize we will never make everyone happy, but if we can change one life by the words we write or the things we say, if we can help the people who need it most and leave the world a better place than we found it, we've done our job.

I've had many experiences in my career where I made significant mistakes but persevered through tough times. For example, I failed my first managerial accounting class and ran for student body president twice, losing both times. Baseball is often seen as a game of failure, but when I reflect on my coaching experiences, I learned to view it as a game of opportunity. Every experience offers a chance to learn a lesson, sometimes the hard way. I'm grateful for the grace that has allowed me to repair and redirect my path.

Three instances of my vulnerability come immediately to mind.

✳ ✳ ✳ ✳

Let's start with the time I almost lost my commission. It was June 2000, and I had just graduated from college and soon after I got married. I was on a field training exercise at Fort Lewis in Washington State for one of my last requirements before commissioning.

It was my wife's birthday, and I was feeling down because I was missing her first birthday celebration as a married couple. Looking back over 20 years later, it seems ridiculous to have felt that way. I accepted an offer from a fellow cadet to use her cellphone, which she wasn't supposed to have, to call my wife and wish her a happy birthday. While my choice to use her cellphone was wrong, it was worse that I denied having it when it was discovered. As a result, I was written up and had to sit in front of a Colonel to plead for forgiveness. That day, I realized I had violated the Army's values by failing to demonstrate selfless service and putting the mission above my desires. This experience reinforced the importance of values and made me a more vigorous advocate for doing the right thing.

Later, I realized I had made someone feel reluctant to come to work. As a First Lieutenant running a port team in Germany, I had a conversation with a warrant officer who entered my office visibly shaken. Because he was nervous, he had prepared everything he wanted to say in writing. He asked me to listen to him entirely before responding, and I agreed.

He expressed his thoughts and feelings candidly, and I found very little to disagree with. I understood his perspective, and it was clear that the environment and culture he described were not what I wanted to foster as a leader. Hearing him out was essential for me to improve the situation.

I am grateful for his honesty, feedback, and courage in choosing to share his feelings with me. This experience often comes to mind as I lead other teams.

My last story is about getting let go from my first job after leaving the military. There were two main reasons for this. First, in 2010, the economic situation was dire, and HR considered me overhead because I wasn't in sales or engineering. Additionally, I was told that I didn't collaborate well with others and tended to work independently. Was that assessment accurate? As someone actively seeking feedback, I conducted a 360-degree review to gauge my core leadership competencies. However, I only piloted it on myself and had no intention of pursuing it further without permission. This perception ultimately made the economic decision easier for my manager.

This story is concluded in the Afterword.

What It Means To Be Vulnerable

> *"Vulnerability is not weakness, and the uncertainty, risk, and emotional exposure we face every day are not optional. Our only choice is a question of engagement."*[71]

Any conversation about vulnerability has to begin with the work of Dr. Brené Brown, who transformed her desire to serve through social work into a career exploring shame, vulnerability, wholeheartedness, and how we as human beings interact with each other.

In her 2012 seminal work, *Daring Greatly: How the Courage to Be Vulnerable Transforms the Way We Live, Love, Parent, and Lead,* she explores how vulnerability unlocks honesty and real connection in our personal and professional lives. It's at the core of all of our most trusted relationships, and it's essential to building an effective, high-functioning team.

Vulnerability Defined

> *"Connection is why we're here. We are hardwired to connect with others, it's what gives purpose and meaning to our lives, and without it there is suffering."*

With these words, Brown lays out the fundamentals of human interaction and contentment:

- We instinctively seek out relationships with others, and we often chart our own happiness by the close family members and friends who understand and accept us — a concept very similar to Glasser's Quality World.

- By contrast, one of the greatest sources of human despair is the fear that, if we were absent, we would not be missed — that somehow we are not worthy of acceptance, or were never truly accepted in the first place.

That's how the natural human desire for connection turns into vulnerability — by the fear of exclusion and rejection. In her 2010 TED Talk, Brown explains this basic psychology underpinning all human interaction[72]:

"So very quickly — really about six weeks into this research — I ran into this unnamed thing that absolutely unraveled connection in a way that I didn't understand or had never seen. And so I pulled back out of the research and thought, I need to figure out what this is. And it turned out to be shame. And shame is really easily understood as the fear of disconnection: Is there something about me that, if other people know it or see it, that I won't be worthy of connection? The things I can tell you about it: It's universal; we all have it. The only people who don't experience shame have no capacity for human empathy or connection. No one wants to talk about it, and the less you talk about it, the more you have it. What underpinned this shame, this 'I'm not good enough' — which, we all know that feeling: 'I'm not blank enough. I'm not thin enough, rich enough, beautiful enough, smart enough, promoted enough.' The thing that underpinned this was excruciating vulnerability. This idea of, in order for connection to happen, we have to allow ourselves to be seen, really seen."

Shame and vulnerability are two sides of the same coin. If vulnerability is the things about ourselves that we fear might cause rejection, shame is the impulse to hide those things and pretend they don't even exist. If you've ever tried to "fake it until you make it," you're probably familiar with vulnerability and shame: This advice recommends that you *pretend* to have experience you don't have, and hope that by the time someone thinks to call you on it, you will have developed that expertise. It's a kind of trickery designed to protect your vulnerabilities.

IN MY OWN LIFE:

FAKE IT 'TIL YOU'RE CAUGHT

Many times I've worked with emerging leaders who admit to having some discomfort being seen in that light. They often feel they don't have sufficient expertise, experience, or relationships to truly be considered "leaders." And in coaching sessions we'll talk about what leadership means to them and many of the preconceived notions of a leader that we're discussing in this book.

In popular culture, the advice given especially to young professionals is to "fake it until you make it." The theory goes, if you can look the part for long enough ("fake it"), even if you don't take actions to develop as a leader, eventually you and others will learn to see yourselves that way ("make it"). Movies like *Tootsie*, *Pretty Woman* and *The Proposal* would have you believe "faking it" is a reasonable pathway to, if not outright success, an outcome you're pretty happy with.

Of course, that's not how real life tends to go. In real life, faking it can lead to disastrous consequences, both for you and your organization.

In 2003, Elizabeth Holmes, then a 19-year-old Stanford dropout, started a health technology company that promised the ability to run multiple diagnostic tests from just a single drop of blood. Theranos quickly became a venture capital darling, and in 2015 had a valuation of $9 billion,[73] based largely on the promises and demeanor of its young founder and CEO. Holmes even had leadership lingo down, as her own notes revealed[74]:

"I am never a minute late. I show no excitement. ALL ABOUT BUSINESS. I am not impulsive. I know the outcome of every encounter. I do not hesitate. I constantly make decisions and change them as needed. I speak rarely. When I do — CRISP and CONCISE. I call bullshit immediately."

Theranos began to unravel in 2018, when the SEC accused Holmes of misleading investors about its capabilities, government contracts, and financial condition, and it was soon revealed the entire premise of the company's success was a charade. Holmes was convicted on four charges of conducting "a yearslong fraud scheme against investors" while CEO of Theranos, and in late 2022 she was sentenced to more than a decade in prison for fraud.[75] But what was so captivating was how she was able to fool the Theranos board of directors, investors, and the world. Linda Neider, chair of the University of Miami Patti and Allan Herbert Business School's Management Department, put it this way[76]:

"Elizabeth Holmes is a fascinating case study of charismatic leadership gone wrong. She possessed many of the classic characteristics that we normally associate with charismatic leaders — a captivatingly optimistic vision of the future, an exceptionally high confidence level, and adept communication skills marked by the ability to modulate her voice and mesmerize others with her piercing eye contact."

The truth is, there is no "fake it until you make it." While some might be born with physical traits often associated with leadership, it is a skill that you can develop — if you choose to do it.

So what do we as aspiring or current leaders do about shame and vulnerability, this idea of not measuring up, of fearing we'll come up short, of worrying about rejection? We typically address that constant anxiety in one of two ways.

The first and most common way is by becoming numb to it[72]:

We live in a vulnerable world. And one of the ways we deal with it is we numb vulnerability. ... The problem is — and I learned this from the research — that you cannot selectively numb emotion. You can't say, here's the bad stuff. Here's vulnerability, here's grief, here's shame, here's fear, here's disappointment. I don't want to feel these. I'm going to have a couple of beers and a banana nut muffin. You can't numb those hard feelings without numbing the other affects, our emotions. You cannot selectively numb. So when we numb those, we numb joy, we numb gratitude, we numb happiness. And then, we are miserable, and we are looking for purpose and meaning, and then we feel vulnerable, so then we have a couple of beers and a banana nut muffin. And it becomes this dangerous cycle.

By compartmentalizing and becoming numb to these anxieties, we hope to feel them less, enough to make it through the day (or year, or career, or life). And it can work. You can in fact train yourself to deny your feelings or dismiss them as unimportant and counterproductive (I did this frequently while in Iraq and upon returning from the combat zone and still struggle with it a bit today). But if you're considering that choice, it's worth also asking if those ends are worth your unhappiness (and ulcers).

We mentioned a second way to address that constant anxiety, and that is by embracing our fears and insecurities and choosing to be vulnerable. Here's how Brown describes those she calls the "whole-hearted," the people who believe they're worthy of love and belonging[72]:

And so these folks had, very simply, the courage to be imperfect. They had the compassion to be kind to themselves first and then to others, because, as it turns out, we can't practice compassion with other people if we can't treat ourselves kindly. And the last was they had connection, and — this was the hard part — as a result of authenticity, they were willing to let go of who they thought they should be in order to be who they were, which you have to absolutely do that for connection.

The other thing that they had in common was this: They fully embraced vulnerability. They believed that what made them vulnerable made them beautiful. They didn't talk about vulnerability being comfortable, nor did they really talk about it being excruciating — as I had heard it earlier in the shame interviewing. They just talked about it being necessary. They talked about the willingness to say, "I love you" first ... the willingness to do something where there are no guarantees ... the willingness to breathe through waiting for the doctor to call after your mammogram. They're willing to invest in a relationship that may or may not work out. They thought this was fundamental.

Yet forging these connections and taking an honest look at our perceived inadequacies invites risk. We open ourselves up to rejection, embarrassment, and the judgment of others. This is as true in our professional lives as it is in our personal ones — after all, every organization is its own society, and the hierarchy of leadership presumes a sort of social contract. And as leaders, the risks of choosing to be vulnerable are that much greater: Our actions are more out in the open, where everyone throughout the organization and even our competitors can judge and second-guess. But the rewards — in terms of personal satisfaction and engagement and the relationships we foster inside and outside the organization — are worth being vulnerable.

The choice to be vulnerable is also essential for fostering psychological safety within teams. Dr. Timothy Clark's research shows that when leaders model vulnerability—admitting mistakes, seeking feedback, and acknowledging limitations—they create inclusion safety, signaling to others that showing up authentically is acceptable and valued.[114] Vulnerability breaks down barriers, encouraging openness, trust, and collaboration. According to Harvard professor Amy Edmondson, teams led by vulnerable leaders report higher levels of engagement, creativity, and performance. [115] Vulnerability also nurtures learner safety by demonstrating that growth requires trial and error, making it safe for others to ask questions and make mistakes without fear of embarrassment or judgment. In this way, the risks leaders take by choosing vulnerability yield rewards beyond personal fulfillment—they foster a culture where psychological safety thrives, empowering team members to contribute their best and drive innovation.

IN MY OWN LIFE:

THE ART OF MESSING UP

During the onset and subsequent couple of years of the COVID pandemic, I collaborated with several leaders trying to balance employee safety with running a business. In my discussions with them, I was repeatedly reminded of the importance of vulnerability. This includes the ability to admit mistakes and to avoid becoming so personally invested in having all the answers that you lose sight of your mission and the welfare of your team.

From a business operations perspective, the pandemic was disruptive in every conceivable way. It presented a health crisis, a staffing crisis, a financial crisis, and a supply and demand crisis. It also created significant challenges for leadership, as the situation was unprecedented and prolonged, lasting what felt like years. In the early stages, there was no playbook for navigating these issues or for effective leadership. With the initial stay-at-home orders extending for over two years, there was no way to avoid the challenges; leaders and employees were facing the reality head-on. Shell-shocked employees looked to their leaders for guidance, while those leaders felt overwhelmed and unsure.

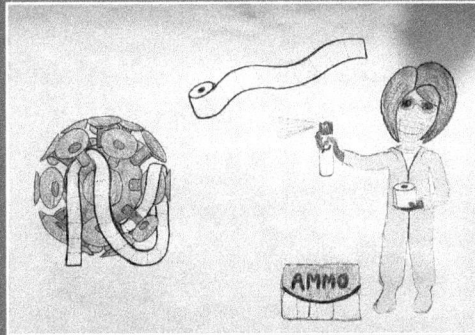

Many decisions made during this time were short-sighted. I've heard several stories of company leaders who dismissed safety concerns just one year into the situation and insisted that everyone return to the office on a specific date—only to find that no one showed up. Employees were hesitant to return, driven by fears for their safety and the success they experienced with the work-from-home model. In one specific case at a company I worked with, it took two-and-a-half years of false starts before employees finally felt safe enough to return to the office.

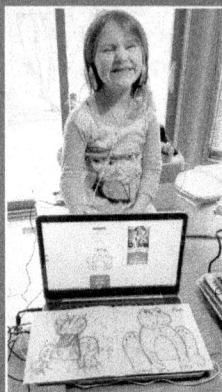

There were other mistakes too — bold predictions that the pandemic would be over in a matter of weeks (only needed fifteen days to slow the spread), creating one-size-fits-all COVID policies (policies that were quite feasible for executives with live-in nannies, far less viable for working moms and dads whose kids were now learning from home). And it wasn't just in the early days of the pandemic — more than two years into the pandemic, it was reported that financial services firms JP Morgan Chase and Goldman Sachs were monitoring ID badge swipes to see how often employees were coming back into the office, causing one employee to complain that "we are treated like children who don't want to do their homework."[77] It's not hard to see how that decision will almost certainly push high-performing employees out the door.

As we continue to learn and lead during challenging times, I want to share the advice I often give my clients: prioritize maintaining strong quality world connections with your teams and staying receptive to their feedback. They need to feel psychologically safe and experience your vulnerability now more than ever.

Choosing To Be a Vulnerable Leader

We've talked about the importance of vulnerability in our personal relationships as well as our professional ones. But what does vulnerability look like in a leader? As one researcher notes[70]:

In this context, vulnerability means breaking down the "professional distance" barrier that we often believe is necessary with our team and colleagues. Instead, it encourages us to build genuine human relationships. Ultimately, this process involves an inward self-awareness journey toward authenticity and sharing your insights with trusted individuals within the organization. It also emphasizes the importance of finding the right balance.

Vulnerability has become an unavoidable part of life, especially as many of us shifted to remote work during and after the pandemic. The lines between "professional life" and "personal life" blurred in this new reality. The sounds of children during virtual meetings, pets walking across desks, neighbors mowing lawns, or spouses unexpectedly entering Zoom calls have become common experiences. These situations reveal our human side, and when leaders embrace this vulnerability, they help create psychological safety, reinforcing Dr. Clark's first stage of psychological safety, Inclusion Safety—where individuals feel accepted and respected for who they are, regardless of imperfections.[114] This acceptance and respect creates an environment where team members feel free to be themselves, knowing they won't be judged for their human moments.

Similarly, the fear of being ridiculed or rejected — illustrated by Kevin Surace's reflection in *Daring Greatly* — mirrors what Dr. Clark describes as a barrier to Challenger Safety.

Kevin Surace, the then-CEO of Serious Materials and *Inc.* magazine's 2009 Entrepreneur of the Year, was asked what the most significant barrier to creativity and innovation was[71]:

"Kevin thought about it for a minute and said, 'I don't know if it has a name, but honestly, it's the fear of introducing an idea and being ridiculed, laughed at, and belittled. If you're willing to subject yourself to that experience, and if you survive it, then it becomes the fear of failure and the fear of being wrong. People believe they're only as good as their ideas and that their ideas can't be seen as too *out there* and they can't *not know* everything.

... Something related to fear keeps people from going for it. They focus on what they already do well, and they don't put themselves out there.'"

People hesitate to share bold or innovative ideas, fearing rejection or shame of being wrong or losing belonging or exclusion from a desired group. Psychological Safety emphasizes that leaders must foster a culture where employees feel safe to question norms and propose new ideas, knowing they won't be dismissed or belittled. Vulnerable leadership — admitting mistakes or embracing not knowing — encourages team members to take these risks, enhancing innovation and collaboration.[71,114]

The truth is, getting the most out of our teams requires connecting with each individual as a person, accepting and being accepted as humans with strengths and weaknesses, moments when we shine and moments when we fail. Earning the trust of your team starts with building relationships and — selectively — identifying opportunities to display and share your vulnerabilities. Brené Brown relates this story from one of her TED Talk presentations[71]:

"During my talk, I asked the audience two questions .... First, I asked, 'How many of you struggle to be vulnerable because you think of vulnerability as weakness?' Hands shot up across the room. Then I asked, 'When you watched people on this stage being vulnerable, how many of you thought it was courageous?' Again, hands shot up across the room.

We love seeing raw truth and openness in other people but are afraid to let them see it in us. … Here's the crux of the struggle: I want to experience your vulnerability, but I don't want to be vulnerable."

Brown's story about audience reactions to vulnerability — where people view others' vulnerability as courageous but struggle to be vulnerable themselves,[71] parallels Clark's insights into Learner Safety. Leaders who display vulnerability, such as admitting they don't have all the answers, send a clear message that mistakes and failure are part of learning. This reduces fear and builds a culture of openness and innovation, inviting team members to ask questions, admit challenges, and experiment without fear that a failure will ultimately end their career.[71,114]

The psychological safety research of Harvard professor Amy Edmondson also aligns with Dr. Clark's principles, reinforcing the connection between vulnerability and psychological safety. Edmondson found that leaders who display vulnerability "get the static out of the way," reducing hesitation and fear within their teams.[116,117] When leaders trust their team by being open about their challenges, they create space for team members to bring forward concerns, admit mistakes, and ask for help without fear of judgment. This builds Contributor Safety, where individuals feel empowered to apply their skills and make meaningful contributions, knowing their efforts will be valued.[71,78]

Ultimately, vulnerability is a powerful tool for building trust and psychological safety within teams. When leaders model vulnerability consistently, they establish a culture where employees feel accepted, encouraged to learn, empowered to contribute, and free to challenge the status quo — leading to stronger relationships, higher engagement, and better team performance.

IN MY OWN LIFE:

PLAY BALL!

When my son was 10 years old, I found myself with an opportunity to manage his baseball team and run the entire baseball organization. At this point in my life, I felt I had much of the experience and transferable skills I would need to run a team and the organization: I owned my own business and had previously worked within organizations, so I already knew how to motivate, set expectations and timelines, communicate, and ask for feedback. Plus, my experience in the military taught me how to lead others and work as a cohesive unit to achieve a goal.

What I lacked, though, was baseball coaching expertise. I knew very little about coaching baseball — sure, I played baseball throughout high school, coached and played softball with my units in the army, and helped my oldest daughter when she played softball. Still, I didn't know about setting up a practice, running drills, or developing baseball talent. (As a leadership coach, I often meet with leaders who understand the technical side of a particular area but not the leadership side. My problem was the reverse: I knew all about leadership and management responsibilities but didn't have the technical expertise to teach twelve 10-year-olds how to throw, hit, and field as exhaustively and effectively as I would have liked.)

I felt I had two options. Option A was the old "fake it until you make it," to be fair, there would be a little of that as I grew into

the role of coach. However, there are three problems with this approach beyond the obvious. First, pretending to have the experience you lack in an athletic setting can be physically dangerous, potentially causing significant injury to the youth athletes you're trying to lead. Second, it builds in the potential for excuse-making: If your lack of familiarity results in poor performance, it becomes very easy to say, "Well, what did you expect?" "Faking it" doesn't relieve you from accountability. Third, it's not easy to fake. Parents are your biggest critics, and if you don't look like you know what you are doing and their son isn't getting better, they move to another organization and your reputation is tarnished.

So, I went with Option B: I acknowledged my limitations and sought to do something about it. I learned everything about leading practices, drills, and a youth baseball team. I researched, read many books, watched hours of coaching videos, and joined groups on social media that freely shared their coaching expertise and knowledge with others to help grow the sport of baseball. I joined the American and Wisconsin Baseball Coaches Association, which gave me access to clinics and some of the country's best high school and college coaches. USA Baseball, the Positive Coaching Alliance, and several others helped me develop my competence and diversify my knowledge. But, perhaps most importantly, I found a mentor to help me with player development, to help me

apply my new knowledge so the youth athletes on my team could grow their skills and I could grow as a coach. This mentor, Dan Gaynor, will have forgotten more about baseball than I will ever know. Dan Gaynor is a former teacher in an area school district and a long-time high school baseball coach. While Coach Gaynor would show me and model the way, he also encouraged me to "write my own book" on coaching baseball. Coach Gaynor humbly encouraged me to build on the base he gave me freely, without any ego or expectation of anything in return, to find my way, style, and process to develop my youth athletes. Coach Gaynor's humbleness and mentorship have allowed me to grow into a confident baseball coach who will pass on his lessons and my lessons and encourage others to write their own books, too.

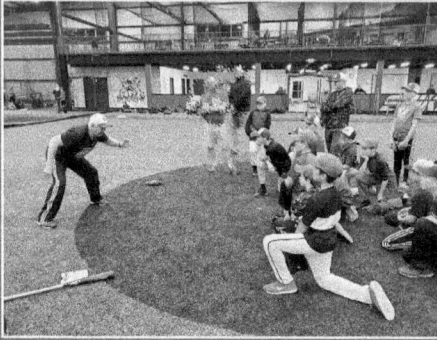

Just as my teams improved, I grew as a coach and a leader, thanks in considerable measure to Coach Gaynor.

This story is concluded in the Afterword.

The Benefits of Vulnerable Leadership

"Trust men and they will be true to you; treat them greatly and they will show themselves great."
— Ralph Waldo Emerson

Similarly, in explaining the importance of trust — the foundation of his Five Behaviors of a Cohesive Team — Patrick Lencioni argues[80] that:

"Trust lies at the heart of a functioning, cohesive team and can only happen when team members are willing to be completely vulnerable with one another. This includes saying things like, 'I'm sorry,' or 'Your idea was better than mine.'"

This concept aligns directly with Inclusion Safety and Learner Safety in Dr. Clark's model of psychological safety.[114] Vulnerability fosters inclusion, allowing individuals to feel accepted and valued for who they are, regardless of mistakes. Leaders who can admit they don't have the answers or ask for help model an essential behavior of learner safety, encouraging others to take risks, ask questions, and grow.

Vulnerable leadership also nurtures Challenger Safety, which is essential for fostering innovation. As studies suggest,[79,81] vulnerability is not a weakness but a strength, empowering leaders to embrace new perspectives and inspiring a culture of curiosity and "collective genius." Dr. Clark's model emphasizes that creativity flourishes when team members feel safe to challenge ideas without fear of retribution. In this environment, employees are encouraged to think critically and propose innovative solutions rather than being told what to do. When leaders demonstrate humility and openness, they not only build trust but also unlock the full potential of their teams, transforming conflict into productive collaboration and driving sustainable success.

Leaders who can admit they don't have the answers, who can be vulnerable enough to ask for help, and who can be open to others' ideas, engage in productive conflict. As one study argues[81]:

Vulnerability is actually a strength for leaders who must admit that tomorrow's answers won't be found in the corner office. Vulnerable leaders incite organizational curiosity, creating a culture of "collective genius." Rather than people being told what to do, they should be inspired about what to think about.

Having this kind of relationship can create lasting inspiration and even loyalty. Consider the following real-life example[70]:

One morning in Bangalore, South India, Archana Patchirajan, founder of a technology startup, called her entire staff in for a meeting. When they were all seated, she announced that she had to let them go because the startup had run out of funds. She could no longer pay them. Shockingly, her staff of high-caliber engineers who had their pick of jobs in the booming Silicon Valley of India, refused to go. They said they would rather work for 50% of their pay than leave her. They stayed and kept working so hard that, a few years later, Archana's company — Hubbl, which provides internet advertising solutions — sold for $14 million. Archana continues to work on startups from the US, and her staff, though thousands of miles away from her, continue to work for her.

What explains the connection and devotion that Archana's staff had toward her? ... When I asked one of Archana's longest-standing employees what drove him and the rest of the team to stay with her, these are some of the things he shared:

- "We all work as a family because she treats us as such."
- "She knows everyone in the office and has a personal relationship with each one of us."
- "She does not get upset when we make mistakes but gives us the time to learn how to analyze and fix the situation."

These quotes indicate that Archana's relationship with her employees goes beyond the typical employer-employee dynamic. She is vulnerable and authentic with them, sharing her doubts candidly during challenging times for the company. Archana does not adhere to a strict hierarchy; instead, she treats her employees like family. She has invested time and emotional resources into building personal relationships with each of them. This vulnerability has fostered an environment rich in psychological safety, allowing them to strengthen their connections and position in each other's quality worlds.

How — and When — To Be Vulnerable

If leaders weren't ready to be vulnerable, COVID certainly forced the issue. And, there was no better time to learn: As leaders, we don't know all the answers, and we certainly didn't when the pandemic hit. But how leaders chose to react to that uncertainty played an outsized role in how their teams — and organizations — were able to respond in the crisis.

Of course, leaders aren't required to be — and shouldn't be — vulnerable all of the time. Leaders need to be confident, aware, alert, and agile to their situations. Part of choosing to be vulnerable is choosing when, with whom, and in what way you give of yourself, with the hope that it will build trust and a deeper connection with the person you're opening up to.

Choosing to Find a Balance

Sharing with someone who will use this information against you, or who isn't interested or ready for that kind of relationship, can backfire, becoming "one more piece of flying debris in an already dangerous storm."[82]

When choosing when and with whom to open up to, ask yourself: How have they responded to this kind of sharing in the past? Are they likely to:

- Feel shame *for* you, confirming how horrified you should be ("You should feel terrible!")?

- Respond with sympathy ("I feel so sorry for you.") rather than empathy ("Oh, I've done that too!")?

- Express disappointment in your imperfections ("I can't believe YOU would do that!")?

- Respond with scolding ("How did you let this happen?")?

- Minimize your shame ("It couldn't have been that bad.")?

- Try to one-up you ("You think that's bad, listen to what happened to me...")?

Instead of sharing everything all at once — especially if you're new to vulnerability — ease into it. Take small risks with people you trust the most. As Brown herself puts it, "share with people who earn the right to hear your story.[82]" I can tell you that personally I am most vulnerable with my wife — she knows all my imperfections and all my mistakes, but she also knows that I can and will persevere.

In My Own Life:

"Why I Changed My LinkedIn Profile Pic"

I recently saw this post on LinkedIn about a leader who had the occasion to rethink her LinkedIn profile picture in the context of a global pandemic. In the corporate world, there is so much pressure to show our best "corporate" selves whenever possible, to the point where we deny our own humanity. I applaud this leader's willingness to embrace her own vulnerability on a social media platform for thousands of friends, colleagues, clients, and strangers to see.

Recently, I took a long hard look at my LinkedIn profile photo — the woman staring back at me had newly highlighted hair and a fresh cut, a pressed blazer, a hint of a smile that showed just the right amount of teeth to let you know she was serious but could be lighthearted when needed. I remember standing in my power pose as my husband snapped the photos. We poured through about 80 shots before we found the one that looked perfectly polished. But the person I was exuding then is not always who I am, and certainly, not who I am right now.

Today's remote world has blurred the lines between my professional and personal selves, so I've chosen to represent that in my photo. Barely dried hair, comfy pullover, ripped jeans — slightly frazzled from having just gotten 3 kids ready for "school" — but smiling and ready for work.

I've witnessed and read enough on authentic leadership to know that being genuine and vulnerable will get you a lot farther in your career than a glossy headshot.

The Choice Theory Perspective on Vulnerability

As you might imagine, William Glasser's idea of the quality world is right in line with Brown's work on vulnerability. Consider his reflections on maintaining quality-world relationships[2]:

Most of us are reluctant to share what is in our quality worlds even with people we are close to because we are afraid they may not support what we want — that they may criticize or ridicule what is so important to us. We know we would choose to feel hurt, angry, or both if they did. ... The best thing to do if you know choice theory is to explain the quality world and what you are afraid of to your partner. This is the way to get trust in a marriage when more is needed. If you don't, your resentment may lead you to criticize and blame your partner, which further reduces the trust."

While here Glasser is talking about a marital relationship, the dynamic is at work in all interpersonal relationships, including those of a leader. And note how they mirror Brown's findings, from fear of ridicule and rejection to embracing vulnerability ("what you are afraid of").

This dynamic can also be seen in Glasser and Glasser's *The Language of Choice Theory,* which contrasts the language of control theory and choice theory in various relationships and situations. In this example, an employee is on the verge of being laid off[3]:

EXTERNAL CONTROL
I'm under pressure from the new owners to cut expenses. I've got to cut two more people. But if you get cut, I don't want you to take it personally.

CHOICE THEORY ALTERNATIVE
I'm under pressure from the new owners to cut expenses. They say I have to cut two more people. I don't have any idea how I'm going to do it. ... I'm talking to each one of you individually. What I want is anything you can think of that might allow me to avoid cutting anyone. ... I want to present to him all we're doing now and possibly could do to cut costs. The way I see it, it's our only chance.

In the external control example, there is no vulnerability or even closeness between the leader and employee. In fact, based on the language he or she uses, it's easy to imagine the employer using the "numbing" tactic Brown describes to keep the discomfort of the situation at arm's length. This choice, though, likely leaves the employee wondering: Are there other options available? Am I a valuable member of this team? Does my manager even value me?

By contrast, the choice theory alternative reflects a strategic decision and an emotional commitment. Rather than detaching from the situation or numbing emotions, the leader becomes actively engaged, signaling inclusion safety by expressing, "This is our best chance" instead of "your best chance." This subtle shift conveys that the employee is a valued part of the solution, fostering a sense of belonging. While the outcome remains uncertain—there's no guarantee the new effort will succeed—the act of vulnerability builds trust, signaling that the leader values the employee beyond transactional performance. This aligns with Dr. Timothy Clark's insights on psychological safety, which creates an environment where the employee is more likely to reciprocate through collaboration rather than disengagement,[114] such as quietly updating their résumé.

This vulnerable approach also opens doors for future conversations, reinforcing learner safety. When leaders are emotionally transparent and demonstrate that they are open to dialogue, they cultivate a culture where ongoing discussions and feedback become natural. Encouraging employees to stay engaged, ask questions, and explore new ideas—even imperfect ones—creates conditions for contributor safety. Leaders who are comfortable admitting their humanity communicate that mistakes are acceptable and part of the path toward continuous improvement.

Consider this thought experiment: Think about the people on your team. You want them fully invested in your organization's success and willing to take risks that foster growth. Would you prefer that they:

- Ask questions, even if it risks making them appear uninformed? Or stay silent, remaining in the dark?

- Share raw, unrefined, or incomplete ideas for potential improvements? Or hold back, sticking to familiar processes?

- Acknowledge their mistakes and grow from them? Or remain confined to their comfort zones, hesitant to broaden their horizons?

Psychologically safe environments encourage precisely this type of engagement. Research by Amy Edmondson and others demonstrates that learning and innovation flourish when team members feel safe to take risks without fear of embarrassment or punishment.[116] If leaders desire this kind of engagement from their teams, the same principles must apply to them. Vulnerable leadership models the behavior they seek, establishing challenger safety by showing that questioning ideas—even their own—is welcome.

Choosing to be vulnerable makes leading more authentic, though not necessarily easier. It requires leaders to surrender to the fact that they, too, are human—flawed, imperfect, and constantly learning. However, this authenticity builds deeper trust and connection, paving the way for stronger teams and more resilient organizations.

Vulnerability bridges leadership and psychological safety, inspiring teams to engage wholeheartedly in the mission, contribute meaningfully, and grow together.

Explore Appendix 5 for further insights into the power of vulnerability and how it can enhance your leadership journey.

C H A P T E R ⑥

CHOOSING TO BE COURAGEOUS

*"Courage is reckoned the greatest of all virtues;
because, unless a man has that virtue, he has no
security for preserving any other."*
— Dr. Samuel Johnson, as quoted by James Boswell

If you're familiar with elements of storytelling, you've probably heard of the "hero's journey." This archetypal story structure revolves around the unlikeliest of heroes overcoming a series of increasingly improbable challenges to achieve a great and noble goal, often for the betterment of society at large. If you can recall a story where a lowly peasant ends up saving the world, odds are you witnessed the hero's journey.

One indispensable element in the hero's journey is performing the courageous act. Toward the end of the story, our hero will inevitably commit to a bold gambit to defeat his arch-nemesis. (In the movies, this typically happens right after a training montage, ideally over an inspirational rock song from the '80s.) In these stories, the hero's courage is demonstrated through an *external* strategy that's built on training, cleverness, and more than a little desperation.

While it's true that making the bold decision in real life requires courage (or perhaps bravery, as we'll discuss later), a true leader's courageous journey starts with a process that is often edited out of the hero's journey — a process of looking *inward*. Consider all the other choices we've discussed:

- The choice to be self-aware, to look inside yourself and confront the parts of your personality you may not be comfortable with.

- The choice to be authentic, to let other people see you just as you are, not just as you want to be seen.

- The choice to be humble, to risk sharing the spotlight — and the acclaim — with others while acknowledging your own flaws and imperfections.

- The choice to be vulnerable, to open yourself up to getting hurt (personally or professionally) in pursuit of closer relationships with your team and others.

Before you have the opportunity to make the bold, external decision, you need to address these internal tests of courageous leadership. In this chapter, we'll talk about what courage is, how to make the courageous decision, and why courage is an essential component of Choice Theory.

What Is Courage?

*"Courage is the first of human qualities because
it is the quality which guarantees the others."*
— *Aristotle*

"Bravery is about a split-second decision — you act without thinking or by external pressure. Courage requires something more profound — it takes heart."[83]

It's surprisingly hard to pin a definition to courage. Many people equate courage with fearlessness — with "looking your enemy in the eye" and "not backing down." But that definition describes an external behavior rather than an internal process, and in doing so falls short. While those actions may be the ones of a courageous individual, I believe courage to be much more than the absence of fear — quite the contrary.

Aristotle, who wrote extensively on the virtue of courage, argues that courage "is a mean with regard to feelings of fear (*phobos*) and confidence (*tharsos*)".[84] Rather than the absence of fear, courage by necessity requires fear to be a main driver of action. Without fear, there is no courage. The narrative continues[84]:

Aristotle begins his account of courage in III.6 by stipulating the sphere of courage, the subject matter of courage, to be fearful things or evils (1115a7). A natural view is that courage may be displayed toward a variety of different objects of fear and in a variety of different contexts.

This makes intuitive sense. For there to be courage, there needs to be an understanding of the potential for meaningful risk or loss — be it a risk to one's life, safety, career, reputation, or any number of other risks. For someone to commit a courageous act, he or she must be genuinely afraid of what might happen should the action fail. A low-stakes act of courage might be asking someone out on a date (risking rejection and humiliation), but if you've been a leader in an organization — or in battle — you know the stakes for a courageous decision can be much higher.

Aristotle's other requisite for courage is confidence, or the reasonable expectation that the action could be successful or have a positive outcome. This is also known as hope[84]:

So Aristotle's claim may be rephrased in the following way. Showing courage is impossible in situations where ... there is also no way to achieve a worthwhile objective. Courageous action requires either hope of safety, or hope of success, or both.

We can add one more component to the definition of courage — that the courageous action is right and noble[85]:

Courageous behaviour [is required to] be directed toward some good which is respected in the community. It is this element which harks back to the concept of the mean in Aristotle's definitions of 'virtue' and 'courage' (2.6.1107a). ... This element, like a number of the others, also includes a dynamic aspect in that courage is "directed" toward good. This establishes a link between courage and integrity, with courage being the executive virtue which is necessary to achieve and maintain organisational integrity.

So let's put it all together. Any difficult decision a leader makes can have a positive or negative outcome:

- The desired, hoped-for goal is usually well established beforehand, as that's typically the impetus for action.

- Fear is often the downside to the action — what loss will occur if the action were to fail (or if only a partial success is achieved).

- Courage, then, is acknowledging that fear — the repercussions of failure — but proceeding because you believe the action is necessary, important, and right. It combines the "morally worthy goal, risk/threat/obstacle, and intentional action."[86]

So rather than fearlessness, courage is the ability to act despite being afraid — or while acknowledging the potential for loss. It's what you use to overcome fear in pursuit of your goal. (Note that you need equal parts hope and fear for there to be courage. A risk-taker who has a lot of confidence but little appreciation for the risks of failure is not acting courageously, nor is the person who acts with no hope of success.)

IN MY OWN LIFE:

TAKING THE LEAP

"Be scared, you can't help that, but don't be afraid."
— *William Faulkner*

Army Airborne school is one of the most prestigious military schools a soldier has the privilege of attending. When I was invited, I agreed knowing full well the risks — in my line of work, few are ever even given the opportunity to join.

The school is located in the heart of Fort Benning, Georgia, where the 250-foot jump towers can be seen from almost every vantage point on the main post. The program lasts three weeks and tests your physical readiness as well as your will, confidence, spirit, and mental toughness.

The first week is ground week, where you are given the Army Physical Fitness Test and instruction on building basic airborne skills. This week we learn the mechanics of jumping and the parachute landing fall, endearingly known as the PLF.

Week 2 begins tower week, where we graduate from a 34-foot tower and the swing lander training to the 250-foot towers. We also learn the basics of exiting the aircraft, counting down until the jump master gives the command for personnel to stand up, hook up, check static lines, check equipment, stand by, and eventually shuffle to the door to exit the aircraft.

In week 3 — jump week — we have gone through all the necessary training and equipment checks, and we are physically ready to go. During jump week, to successfully earn your airborne wings, you must complete five successful jumps at 1,250 feet from a C130 or C17 aircraft, some without combat equipment but most with.

I successfully completed all three weeks and my five jumps to earn the airborne qualification badge which was presented to me on the drop zone after my final jump. Yet, despite all this preparation, many of us might have been scared (who wouldn't, jumping 1250 feet above ground from a moving aircraft?). There were several in my "chalk" that failed to jump because fear froze them. Even after the jump master gave them a second chance, they refused to exit the aircraft.

My goal was for a successful jump and landing, earning the coveted airborne wings and proving to myself I could overcome any physical and mental stress. The fear, of course, was

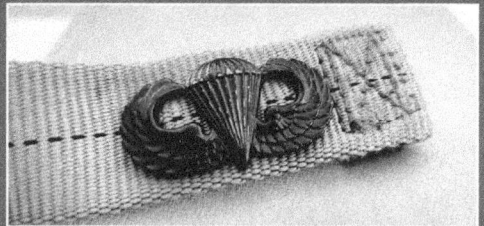

that through equipment failure or — more likely — a failure on my part to execute my training, I was going to turn into a human pancake in Fort Benning, Georgia.

But I had the hope and confidence in my training, equipment, and the professionals that surrounded me, and that allowed me to have courage to successfully jump from the plane. In this case, overcoming my fear required a literal leap of faith.

Dr. Samuel Johnson calls courage the "greatest of all virtues" in that it underpins all the others. The leadership choices discussed in this book are all virtues built on courage: In each instance, leaders have to make a courageous choice, often at personal or professional risk, with the hope that on the other side of that choice lies a closer connection in their relationships. Let's look at these choices through the lens of courage.

Courage and Self-Awareness

"Leadership must start from within — from within the leader's heart — where real courage resides."[87]

It may feel counterintuitive to think you need courage to sit alone and reflect. Yet that's exactly what is necessary when evaluating your fears, needs, self-doubts, and faults.

Leaders tend to self-identify as, if nothing else, capable and competent. While they might not say they're perfect, they certainly tend to focus more on what they can do than what they can't. Yet there's a lot to be gained by examining where you fall short, and the choice to *meaningfully* acknowledge your limitations and flaws is not an easy one. Ask yourself the following questions and consider journaling your answers:

- What are your flaws, as a person and a leader? Can you list them without downplaying them or dismissing them as "that's just who I am"?

- In what ways could your flaws significantly impact your ability to lead?

- What was an instance when an action you took turned out to be wrong, you admitted it publicly, and you were able to course correct?

- In what ways can you improve as a leader, no matter how uncomfortable the process might make you?

- What are ways in which you can solicit honest, candid feedback from people you work with — not only from peers, but from those you report to and those who report to you?

If taken seriously, the journey of self-awareness can be uncomfortable and difficult. It can pierce your ego and cause your confidence to waver. It's far easier to skip the journey entirely or minimize the seriousness of your limitations as a leader. Yet growth requires you have the courage and maturity to look deeply at who you are as a leader and as a person, as did Martin Parkinson, Australia's Secretary of the Department of the Prime Minister and Cabinet[88]:

Being bold is also about daring to put your own assumptions and biases under the microscope, and if that process of introspection [becoming self-aware] reveals you've come up short, it means being courageous enough to commit to a new course.

Back when I was Secretary of the Treasury, the leadership group and I came face-to-face with the uncomfortable reality that Treasury's lack of diversity was largely a product of our own — and my own — biases.

Too often, we found our focus on recruiting on merit meant looking for someone who had done the job before and could therefore do it again — a safe pair of hands. It just so happened that the only candidates ticking this box tended to look, sound and think like those of us already in Treasury. The fault wasn't the concept of merit, but how we perceived merit.

In the years since, I've made it a personal priority to not just say that I'm a champion of diversity and leave it at that, but actually be persistent in holding myself and the people I lead accountable for change.

In any role, it's far easier to keep your blinders on and focus only on the task at hand, instead of the assumptions and thought processes you go through to accomplish that task. Your willingness to even acknowledge your biases and consider how they're affecting your decision-making is a courageous act, and more often than not, acting on that insight leads to reward on the other side.

In the Army, we have something called "the 20% solution," based on Pareto's 80/20 rule. Whenever I arrived at a new unit or location, I knew from experience that our mission was not like a math problem from school, where you're given upfront all the information you need to solve the problem. In any given assignment, we rarely had a completely clear picture of all the variables and parameters at play. At best, we would have 20% of the relevant facts laid out for us, with 80% to be determined by the situation on the ground and by new developments as they arose over the course of the mission. That required making decisions without having all the relevant data and perspective: You had to use what information you had and improvise as conditions changed.

Whether you're leading a battalion, a bakery, or a small team, you're never going to have a complete picture of the problem (or problems) at hand, and there will be times when you'll never know if the decisions you made were the correct ones, even with years of hindsight. Leadership requires making the best of that 20% with the information you do have, and that starts with understanding what about yourself is informing your decisions. Lacking information can be frustrating, but you can't let a lack of information, or a denial of your own behavior, be an excuse to act shortsightedly.

Have the courage to look inward. Have the courage to ask questions. Take stock of your strengths and your weaknesses, and plan accordingly. (For example, do you tend to disengage or shut down when you get stressed and look for the easiest solution? What can you do now to make better decisions in the future?) The process can be uncomfortable, but it will make you a better leader.

Courage and Authenticity

> *"It takes a lot of courage to break the mold of leadership and lead in a way that is authentic to you, but it's what the world desperately needs. We can't change the landscape of business and leadership unless we start having the courage to be who we really are."*[89]

On the surface, authenticity doesn't seem like something that would require a lot of courage. After all, from a young age, we're often told to "just be yourself" (more on that later). However, that advice is quickly forgotten as we mature and grow, in school and especially in our careers. Instead, we learn that to fit in a desired social or professional network, we need to appear and act in a way we feel will be acceptable to the larger group. We sacrifice authenticity for acceptance.

This is especially true when it comes to leadership. While leading may take out-of-the-box thinking, to be viewed as a leader, we often revert to imitating how we think leaders should look and behave, or fall back to professional or even gender stereotypes. In the process, we often strip ourselves of our personality and "close up," walling off personal and professional relationships to create a cool, professional distance, as we discussed earlier.

What does that accomplish? While it might feel like you're being more leader-like, in reality you're artificially imposing barriers in your quality world. You forge superficial relationships, and you limit how much the people you lead can become personally engaged with you and the organization. After all, it's hard to bond with or even trust someone you don't feel like you know, or with someone you feel doesn't trust you enough to be themselves.

Instead, have the courage to bring your whole self to your role as a leader. Allow yourself the freedom to be human. Go beyond what you might normally do and *invite* people to get to know you personally. Becoming a better leader starts with choosing to be a better person. That takes courage!

A good example is the leader who has to lay off one (or more than one) of his or her direct reports. You essentially have two approaches to this difficult conversation. The first is to be "business-like": direct, somewhat aloof, apologetic perhaps, but still detached — pretty much, get the conversation over with as quickly as possible. But what message does that send? That you and the organization do not really care about your direct reports? That your own discomfort means more than the well-being of the person getting dismissed?

The courageous leader can instead choose to bridge that discomfort and show the direct report respect and love by speaking authentically with candor, honesty, and compassion. By choosing to be present in a potentially emotional moment — yes, one where the direct report may express feelings of fear, anger, and blame toward the organization generally and you specifically — you are validating the relationship and showing concern, human being to human being. At all times, leaders put the people they lead first — even at the end of their relationship.

A final but important note about authenticity: "Being authentic" is not meant to justify doing whatever you want under the guise of "just being yourself." Brown argued[90] that such a take on authenticity misconstrues what authenticity is really about. Instead:

Authenticity takes courage. The core of authenticity is the courage to be imperfect, vulnerable, and to set boundaries. ... Authenticity requires almost constant vigilance and awareness about the connections between our thoughts, emotions, and behaviors. It also means staying mindful about our intentions. Real authenticity actually requires major self-monitoring, which is courageous ... it's thinking about what you're sharing, why you're sharing it, and with whom you should be sharing it.

It's not about doing whatever you want while saying "I'm just being me" — there's no courage in that. Choosing to be authentic is about understanding why you think, feel and act the way you do, and acting with the knowledge of how those things influence your decisions and relationships.

Let's close this section out with Brown[90]:

We need braver, more authentic leaders. We need cultures that support the idea that vulnerability is courage and also the birthplace of trust, innovation, learning, risk-taking, and having tough conversations.

None of those positive qualities mentioned at the end of that quote — trust, innovation, learning, risk-taking, and having tough conversations — exists without courage.

IN MY OWN LIFE

KAYLEE'S STAND AGAINST INJUSTICE AND RETALIATION

After I published the first edition of *Where Leadership Begins*, a story about Kaylee arrived in my inbox. Inspired by Martha's tale of courage (IMOL on page 188), Kaylee felt compelled to stand up for her values and principles. Her story is a powerful example of choosing courage in the face of injustice. She didn't wait for the "perfect" moment to take action; instead, she spoke up, fully aware of the potential consequences even when challenging. Here is Kaylee's story:

✶ ✶ ✶ ✶

Kaylee shuffled the papers on her desk, a familiar weight pressing down on her. For months, she had been juggling her job and half the responsibilities of a younger, less-experienced colleague, a burden made heavier by the knowledge that her younger colleague was paid more. It was demoralizing, but worse than the unfair workload was the uncomfortable truth she could no longer ignore: their manager, Goeff, treated the young co-worker more like a daughter than an employee, excusing her from responsibilities and dismissing Kaylee's repeated concerns. This was the injustice Kaylee faced, a situation that many of us can relate to in our own lives.

Despite her efforts to raise the issue with Goeff, nothing had changed. Every conversation ended similarly, with Goeff brushing off her frustrations and saying, "She's still learning. Give her time," or that he agreed with an issue and that he would take care of it, only not to do much of anything. The favoritism was apparent and unfair. Kaylee's experience and dedication were being overlooked in favor of a co-worker who didn't carry her weight.

Kaylee's growing suspicion that age discrimination was at play deepened the sting of injustice. But she wasn't one to back down. She knew she had a choice: remain silent and tolerate the unfair treatment or find the courage to speak up, even if it meant putting herself in a vulnerable position.

<u>Speaking Truth to Power</u>

The situation became even more troubling as Kaylee observed a troubling dynamic between the parish priest, Fr. Aron, and her younger colleague. Their interactions were becoming increasingly personal, with extended hours in each other's offices, interacting only with each other at public events, and questionable outside work interactions and activities raised uncomfortable questions about boundaries. The perception of an inappropriate emotional relationship, and perhaps more, was spreading throughout the workplace, creating suspicion and scandal among parish and school staff, parishioners, and board members. No one wanted to address the issue—gossiping quietly was easier than confronting the priest directly. But Kaylee couldn't ignore what she saw. At a minimum, what appeared to be an inappropriate emotional relationship was casting a shadow over the parish and priest's integrity, and the favoritism toward her younger colleague by both Goeff and Fr. Aron undermined morale.

Knowing the risks, Kaylee decided to confront the situation head-on. She requested a private meeting with Fr. Aron and Danny, the Director of Administrative Services (which is like Human Resources and Finance at a Catholic parish), her heart pounding as she rehearsed what she wanted to say. She knew the conversation could have consequences—Fr. Aron and Danny held considerable power in the parish—but staying silent wasn't an option.

When the meeting began, Kaylee spoke calmly but firmly.

"Father, I want to share a concern I've been having," she began. "There's a growing perception among staff about your relationship with [her colleague]. I know that perception isn't always reality, but how things appear affects the parish's reputation, the volunteers I work with, parish and school staff, and your ability to lead. I think it's important to address this before it causes more harm."

After presenting Fr. Aron with all the evidence and sharing conversations others had with her and how Goeff was handling her colleague's poor performance issues, his face hardened, his mouth narrowed, and his brow furrowed. Fr. Aron denied any wrongdoing, but the air between them thickened with tension. It was clear he didn't appreciate being questioned or given any feedback. Danny sat there with nothing to say, out of shock or guilt, because he knew what was happening between Fr. Aron and the younger colleague.

"That's a dangerous assumption to make, Kaylee," he said sternly, angered. "I suggest you be careful about where you direct your attention. I am coaching her!" he said threateningly.

Kaylee held his gaze, her hands trembling slightly under the table. But she didn't back down. "I'm not making accusations. I'm saying that, as the parish leader, you need to be mindful of how your actions are perceived, especially as a Catholic priest—and, as importantly, by our staff, school, and community. It creates suspicion and scandal, affecting everyone's work and contributions."

She knew the risk she had taken by speaking up to someone as influential as Fr. Aron, but she also knew that doing what was right often came with consequences.

The Cost of Courage

Soon after she met with Fr. Aron, Kaylee began to feel the weight of retaliation. The Director of Administrative Services, Danny, who worked closely with Fr. Aron and Goeff, started to put undue pressure on her, which made it evident they didn't want her to be employed there any longer. Meanwhile, Goeff continued to favor the younger co-worker, excusing her from key responsibilities and turning a blind eye to Kaylee's growing frustration and her colleague's scandalous relationship with Fr. Aron.

Kaylee knew what was happening—she was being punished for speaking up. The environment became increasingly hostile, with Goeff and Danny undermining her efforts and dismissing her contributions. They even dismissed her colleague's verbal attack and tantrum in a team meeting. There were moments when Kaylee wondered if she should walk away. After all, it felt like the deck was stacked against her.

But quitting wasn't in her nature. Despite the challenges, Kaylee remained committed to her work and those who relied on her. She chose to stay, not for the recognition she would never receive, but because she believed in doing what was right and humbly put the community above herself. Her courage and resilience in the face of adversity is truly inspiring.

Each day, she continued to deliver high-quality work, even as the toxic environment around her tried to wear her down. She ensured her work for the parish ran smoothly, took care of the tasks her co-worker neglected, and focused on serving the parish community despite feeling undervalued and overlooked.

Quiet Courage and Lasting Impact

Kaylee's courage wasn't just in confronting Fr. Aron's scandalous relationship or addressing Goeff's pseudo-father-daughter relationship with her colleague — it was in how she showed up every day, doing the job no one recognized with grace and professionalism. She knew that authentic leadership wasn't about titles or power — it was about integrity, about staying true to her values, even when no one was watching. It was about humility in putting the good of the community ahead of her own.

Though she never received an apology or acknowledgment from her superiors, her quiet strength didn't go unnoticed by the volunteers she was responsible for leading. Her closest team members saw how she carried the weight of two jobs without complaint and stood up for what was right, even at a personal cost.

"Kaylee kept the programs running when no one else would," one team member said privately. "She could have given up, but she didn't. That takes real courage."

While Kaylee stood in the fire, favoritism and toxicity took root. She remained true to her values, even though they forced her to separate from the work she loved and where she inspired many.

Lessons from Kaylee's Courage

When Kaylee faced retaliation, she didn't allow it to break her spirit. Instead, she chose to rise above it by focusing on what she could control: the quality of her work and her commitment to doing what was right.

Kaylee's story highlights that courage isn't always manifested through grand gestures. Sometimes, it simply involves showing up each day with integrity, even when it seems like no one is paying attention. It's about holding firm to your values, even when you feel alone and unsupported. Courage is not the absence of fear; rather, it is the choice to act despite it.

Kaylee's leadership shines as an example for all of us: We don't need a title to lead—we only need the courage to do what's right, especially when it's hard. Through her actions, she proved that even in the most challenging environments, leadership begins with the choices we make every day.

Courage and Humility

"We all have blind spots that impact the way we interact with others. Unfiltered 360-degree feedback is not always easy to hear, but it can breathe new life into your relationships and leadership style if you listen and act."[91]

Humility, real humility, is not a characteristic we typically associate with leaders. Although people tend to like leaders who can be self-deprecating, the act of selecting a leader often becomes a popularity contest. We typically prefer leaders who are the most self-assured, attractive, and charismatic. Choosing to be humble, to de-emphasize one's sense of importance, feels almost paradoxical.

However, for those leaders who recognize the importance of putting the team and greater organization above themselves, the courageous choice to be humble is also a crucial one[92]:

Humility is a core quality of leaders who inspire close teamwork, rapid learning and high performance in their teams, according to several studies in the past three years. Humble people tend to be aware of their own weaknesses, eager to improve themselves, appreciative of others' strengths, and focused on goals beyond their own self-interest. In fact, leadership effectiveness is highly correlated to a leader's approach to learning, versatility, and their desire to continually learn.[111]

Yet for all of these benefits, humility isn't something leaders or would-be leaders readily embrace. In reality, the choice to be humble requires a great deal of courage — we risk forgoing personal recognition (potentially in the forms of power, money, career advancement) in sharing credit, acknowledging blame and putting others first. Choosing to be humble is also at the heart of putting aside your pride (as we saw in the choice to be vulnerable) and risking your professional reputation for the betterment of the organization. It can be seen in all kinds of courageous behaviors:

- Asking questions, even if it means putting your ignorance on display

- Unlearning and relearning something you are really good at

- Owning up to mistakes

- Putting forth unpopular ideas when those ideas are necessary

- Encouraging people to disagree with you in pursuit of better solutions

- Standing up to peers and superiors, knowing that you might be wrong — or aware that even if you're right, you risk blowback from superiors

- Seeking out others to provide you with their wisdom, experience, and perspectives

- Closing your mouth and opening your mind and ears to listen

IN MY OWN LIFE:

RECALLING MY ALDERMAN

Often what keeps us from making the difficult choice is the potential consequences — we might know the right and moral thing to do but are afraid of how the results could impact us individually. But I've found that sometimes it's not the consequences you feel that can make a choice difficult — it's when the choices you make invite those consequences upon others.

✶ ✶ ✶ ✶

In the winter of 2020, I faced this situation in my own life. The city where I live was recently represented by an official the state's largest newspaper called "one of the city's highest-profile aldermen." Unfortunately, this person was not living up to the responsibilities of elected office in several respects — some technical (violations of city residence statutes), some professional (inappropriate behavior that prompted his removal from committee assignments), some personal (harassment of one of his constituents), and some legal (four criminal counts, including a felony charge, tied to an alleged domestic abuse incident).

But politics being what they are, he had a lot of supporters, and I had a decision to make. On the one hand, he was abusing his position as alderman, and the people in my city deserved better representation than what they were getting. On the other hand, in today's society, taking public action like initiating a recall would have invited threats and harassment — not just to me, but to my family, my baseball family, and my business.

Ultimately, I decided the greater public good needed to take precedence over my fears. After consulting with some of the people who my decision would have impacted — and after the alderman refused both private and public pleas to resign — I chose to co-chair a committee to recall the alderman with another concerned citizen, Mike Walsh.

The recall process was highly charged, to say the least. Many thought it was a political hit job, retribution for switching parties when he ran for state assembly (clearly not the case). In getting the required community signatures, we encountered a lot of hostility, both on social media and in person. We initiated the recall in the middle of winter, Christmas was approaching, and COVID was rampant, but we forged on knowing we deserved better than the person occupying the seat despite the conditions. Knowing what we were up against and all-too-aware that recalls rarely work as intended, we proceeded anyway in the best interest of our community.

Ultimately our efforts proved successful: We obtained over 54% of the signatures we needed in just eight days, overcoming several doors slammed in our faces, sub-zero windchills, snow, and a COVID-weary community. With the alderman's walls closing in on him, he elected to resign and sought treatment for his issues. We now have an upstanding citizen as our new alderman who humbly puts his community first above any political aspirations.

Humility shouldn't be perceived as a weakness. When you have the courage to be humble and put aside your pride, you develop the strength to be straightforward and not feel the need to please everyone. Consider these findings from Hogan Assessments[93]:

Humble leadership should not be confused with weak leadership. For instance, humble leaders may listen to others and consider alternate viewpoints, resulting in a more beneficial decision. Humble leaders can (and should) demonstrate confidence, show assertiveness, and set forth a clear vision for the organization.

Let's conclude this section with a final thought on the courageous and humble leader[91]:

Courageous leaders refuse to hide behind jargon and wiggle-words — they use straight-talk and are not afraid to say "I don't know." They also share information instead of hoarding it. And they are not afraid of learning new things.

At its core, humble leadership does not focus on making sure you get the credit you feel you deserve or seek to avoid blame. It moves beyond pride and gets to what's truly best for the organization.

Courage and Vulnerability

"Courage is courage is courage. Courage is when you put your ass on the line literally, figuratively, or otherwise."
— Ryan Holiday

Courage is acting in the face of fear. Sitting with the discomfort but working through it, not around it. Showing up fiercely and completely, bringing your vulnerabilities, imperfections and inadequacies, but not being driven by them.[94]

Take a moment to think about what's being asked of a leader. We previously discussed the difference between managing and leading — maintaining the status quo versus taking your team or organization from where it is now to where it could be in the future. Leading is bringing about change in the face of an unknowable future, often using only your experience and judgment as your guide.

When you're a leader, you're often expected to know exactly what that future looks like and anticipate all the problems your team will encounter on the way (as well as how to solve them). Do you have the courage to tell people who look up to you or peers that you don't have the answers? What about the executives of your organization? What about shareholders? What if you make a mistake?

Consider this example from Bill George, CEO of Medtronic and author of *Authentic Leadership: Rediscovering the Secrets To Creating Lasting Value*[95]:

In my first year as CEO of Medtronic, I passed up the opportunity to buy a rapidly growing angioplasty company because it faced patent and pricing risks. While those risks proved valid, Boston Scientific bought the company instead, transforming both enterprises and creating a formidable competitor for Medtronic. I didn't have the courage to accept short-term risk to create long-term gain. It took Medtronic two decades of expensive research and development programs and additional acquisitions to become the leader in this field.

Leaders are, first and foremost, human beings. They make mistakes. They have errors in judgment. And, while not forgoing accountability, acknowledging the parts of yourself that you want to hide, and sharing those parts with others, comes with risk — risk for ridicule, risk for demotion, risk that you disappoint people who look up to you. But with that risk comes an opportunity to forge meaningful connections that are at the core of every good leader's relationships.

Is this process of examining and acknowledging our vulnerabilities uncomfortable? If done right, absolutely. But when you're a leader, you can't be afraid of discomfort. In his seminal book *Tribes: We Need You to Lead Us,* Seth Godin argues[96] that rather than run from the things that make us feel small, leaders should seek out those moments:

Leadership is scarce because few people are willing to go through the discomfort required to lead. The scarcity makes leadership valuable. ... It's uncomfortable to stand up in front of strangers. It's uncomfortable to propose an idea that might fail. It's uncomfortable to challenge the status quo. It's uncomfortable to resist the urge to settle. When you identify the discomfort, you've found the place where a leader is needed. If you're not uncomfortable in your work as a leader, it's almost certain you're not reaching your potential as a leader.

It's easy for leaders to consider fear and doubt to be your greatest enemies. But aren't they also your greatest allies if they teach you to explore what about you is causing you to feel that way? If you take the time for a bit of authentic soul-searching, fear and doubt might lead you to insights you haven't fully considered.

IN MY OWN LIFE:

MARTHA'S STORY

Courage and fear are two sides of the same coin. When you choose to make the courageous act, you're choosing to acknowledge and embrace your fear for some greater outcome, with full knowledge that doing so incurs some measure of risk. Some of the stories I shared in this book talk about the risk of incurring physical harm, be it from driving through the war-torn streets of Baghdad to jumping out of a plane.

But when we choose to let others into our quality worlds, we're opening ourselves to a more emotional kind of risk — the risk of rejection, the risk of being let down, the risk of our letting other people down, the risk of breaking norms others adhere to. I'd like to turn this narrative over to a close friend, who here I'll call Martha, as she recounts a time she summoned the courage to fire an employee.

✶ ✶ ✶ ✶

Many years ago, I served in a community coordinator role within my organization and had approval to hire an assistant. Tina had previously volunteered for a colleague, so I was already somewhat acquainted with her, and her interview went very well. I found her to be much like me — an outgoing people-person, characteristics that are needed for this client-facing position. Our team looked at other candidates as well, but all of us agreed she was the best one for this position.

In the beginning, things were great: Tina communicated well and ably fulfilled the responsibilities of her job description. Problems started when I became pregnant with my third child. Tina had previously shared that she and her husband were struggling to start a family, and I was very conscious of that fact when I shared my news with her. And she was excited and joyous at first.

Unfortunately, her behavior started to change as the months went on. She kept trying to involve herself in the personal details of my pregnancy, even mapping out the fastest routes to the hospital (not the hospital I had chosen) should I have gone into labor during work. She overstepped her boundaries professionally too, at one point telling me how much she resented my becoming pregnant. She also started second-guessing my decisions, secretly going over my head when she didn't like a course of action I chose. It made the office atmosphere increasingly awkward and tense, so much so that I felt I needed to start documenting her behavior.

After one event, post-maternity leave, in which Tina continually resisted my authority, I decided I had enough. It was time to let Tina go.

This was a challenge for me, for multiple reasons. Firing Tina would be logistically difficult: Ours was a small, close-knit organization, and Tina and her family were very well-liked. (Our organization's hiring choices were largely based on culture and who you knew in the work community, not necessarily how qualified you were — so to let someone go would be seen by some members as a slap in the face and put a strain on the organization.) It would also mean losing the only administrative support I had.

Plus, I didn't know how everyone affected would react. What would Tina do? Would she become aggressive? Would she retaliate somehow? What about the community or her colleagues? Would they choose Tina's side over my own? Would this affect my own prospects to advance in my career?

But even more than that, it was challenging personally. It felt like admitting to a failure on my part — a failure to adequately evaluate candidates, a failure to give Tina the tools and knowledge she needed to succeed, a failure to help her grow into her role. I felt I was letting everyone down — Tina, the organization, myself. I also felt badly for what Tina and her husband were going through, and had to own the fact that my choice to terminate her employment would make their lives harder.

For a natural-born people-pleaser like myself, admitting and confronting this mistake struck at who I was as a person.

In spite of those fears, I decided I needed to act. My relationship with Tina was damaged beyond repair, which affected me personally as well as my ability to serve my organization. Moreover, I had serious concerns my relationship with her would deteriorate further after my daughter was born and I was working while raising a newborn.

In the end, I did fire her soon after coming back from maternity leave. And as much as I would like to say my fears were overblown, the truth is, some of those negative outcomes I worried about came to pass. (I suppose that's part of courage — it's not just overcoming your fears, but also acknowledging the consequences of your courageous and well-intentioned act.)

Just the same, I felt then — and still now, years later — that firing Tina was the right decision. It was uncomfortable at the time, but looking back, it also helped me grow, both as a person and a leader.

This story is concluded in the Afterword.

They can also be used to build relationships. In *Daring Greatly,* Brené Brown recounts[71] just such an instance when she spoke to undergraduates about discomfort, vulnerability, and courage:

"During the Q&A session after my talk, one of the students asked me a question that I'm sure is often on the minds of people when I talk about vulnerability. He said, 'I can see how vulnerability is important, but I'm in sales and I don't get what that looks like. Does being vulnerable mean that if a customer asks me a question about a product and I don't know the answer, I just say what I'm thinking: "I'm new and I really don't know what I'm doing?"' ... My answer was no. And yes. In that scenario, vulnerability is recognizing and owning that you don't know something; it's looking the customer in the eye and saying, 'I don't know the answer to that, but I'll find out. I want to make sure you have the correct information.' I explained that the unwillingness to engage with the vulnerability of not knowing often leads to making excuses, dodging the question, or — worst-case scenario — bullshitting. That's the deathblow in any relationship, and the one thing I've learned from talking to people who sell for a living is that sales is all about relationships."

For many leaders, admitting you don't have all the answers and that you still have things to learn requires an immense amount of courage. It feels like you're putting your credibility as a leader and as a person on the line. But as we saw in Brown's anecdote, avoiding the question — or, worse, making up an answer out of whole cloth — can do far more damage to your reputation.

Forgive and Forget?

> *"Everyone says forgiveness is a lovely idea,*
> *until they have something to forgive."*
> — C. S. Lewis

There's one last point I want to make on the subject of courage and vulnerability. You've likely heard the phrase "forgive and forget." It's such a short, commonly used axiom that we often forget how hard it is to put into practice in real life.

In the "forgive and forget" dynamic, the act of forgiveness, by itself, does not require a lot of courage. Yes, it does require acknowledging and overcoming a personal injury, but an injury that occurred *in the past* — it's recognizing a past injury and letting it go. By comparison, courage concerns itself with the present and the future — it may be required to take an action in the present to hopefully achieve some future benefit.

So the "forgive" half of the equation does not involve a lot of courage. What we do *after* forgiving — that's where courage comes in.

When there is an injury that requires forgiveness, most of us — even those of us who choose to forgive — will not forget under the guise of pragmatism. While we might ultimately get over the injury, we certainly don't want to experience it again, in the same way we might learn to not touch a burning stove. We therefore make a point to file the incident away and let it influence the relationship going forward.

It's worth understanding exactly what that does, though. While "forgiving but not forgetting" may provide some protection from future harm, it also starts us down the road to removing the other person from our quality world. It's trading intimacy for safety, allowing the breach of trust to become a barrier to creating a closer relationship.

And there's more to not-forgiving and not-forgetting than just the pragmatic. If you've ever been (or even felt) wronged, you've probably experienced the thrill of victimhood, a sort of "moral superiority" that many people find intoxicating. One researcher describes this sense of power this way[97]:

So why do you hang onto your anger? Frankly, you get a kick out of it. Anger feels empowering because you "get" to feel wronged. … Anger lets you shut out dialogue and alternate views just as effectively as if you were putting a headset on your ears and filling them with a loud playlist full of self-righteousness. Bitterness bolsters your sense of yourself as "right." Being right just feels weirdly good.

So what if we choose to forgive *and* forget — to forgive the breach of trust and be willing to move past it without letting it impact the relationship?

To forgive and forget requires the courage to risk a further injury, but it has the upside that a leader needs — a closer relationship and opportunity for growth. (This has been called TRUST Courage: "The courage of confidence in others — letting go of the need to control situations or outcomes, having faith in people and being open to direction and change."[98]) It doesn't mean that every wrong needs to be forgiven — sometimes the healthiest and most courageous choice is to remove someone from your quality world, to neither forgive nor forget. And even if you choose to "forgive and forget," that doesn't mean you ignore the original offense, and a leader absolutely should take steps to ensure the other person has an opportunity for growth and redemption.

But when that opportunity for learning has taken place, it means having the courage and maturity to let go of the original offense as if it never happened and to trust again, wholeheartedly. Yes, that requires a leap of faith, of sorts, but if you've ever received the benefit of a second chance, you know the rush of gratitude and grace that accompanies an opportunity to atone for past mistakes.

When To Be Courageous

"Courage is not waiting for your fear to go away;
it is confronting your fear head-on."[99]

How do you know if your courageous act is the right decision? How do you know *when* to be courageous?

Knowing when to take a calculated risk, when the bold choice is the right one, is a skill leaders need to, and can, learn. That kind of judgment is developed through one of the previous choices you've made — the choice to be self-aware.

Before committing to a courageous action, leaders need to understand *why* they're doing it. Is it in pursuit of your organization's goals? Is it to increase your standing within the organization? Is it to adhere to your own personal beliefs? Is it made in the spur of the moment, or after careful consideration? Your reasons behind your decision-making will shed some light on the rightness of the decision.

One researcher believes[100] "most great business leaders teach themselves to make high-risk decisions" by learning what she calls the "courage calculation." The courage calculation requires leaders to ask themselves several questions before committing to the courageous choice:

- *What are my goals?* Determine if your goals are attainable, ethical, and moral.

- *How important are my goals?* A courageous choice involves personal or professional risk. Before committing to it, ask yourself if the goal is worth the risk.

- *Do I have a supportive power network?* How strong are your relationships with your direct reports, peers, and other influencers within the organization?

- *What are the trade-offs?* Consider the following matrix:

In Appendix 6, you will have the opportunity to explore the Courageous Decision Guide further and identify areas for greater courage in your work and life.

If You Choose To Act Courageously	If You Decline To Act Courageously
What are the benefits to you? These could be physical, financial, emotional, political, interpersonal, etc.	*What are the benefits to you?* What do you gain from playing it safe?
What are the risks to you? What damage could be done through your action — physical, financial, reputational, etc.	*What are the risks to you?* The safer course is not without risk. If the courageous choice is the right one, where would that leave you?
What are the benefits to others? How might the courageous choice impact your team or larger organization? (Remember, leadership is about change.)	*What are the benefits to others?* How might others benefit from your choice not to act?

What are the risks to others? Are you setting others up for failure? What are the opportunity costs if your courageous choice is incorrect?	*What are the risks to others?* Does your decision impact those around you?

In considering the tradeoffs, be honest about the pros and cons. Imagine an all-too-familiar situation where one member of the team is not up to the responsibilities of their job, and the team takes the path of least resistance — by working around her or absorbing her responsibilities into their own. If you manage this employee, you have a decision to make: to address the issue or ignore it. If you ignore it, you avoid an uncomfortable conversation (or series of conversations) but hamper the team. If you choose to be courageous, you expose yourself to personal risk of discomfort, but *benefit* the team. Laying out the pros and cons against the responsibilities of your role can help lead you to the right decision.

1. *Is now the time to act?* Is this an emergency? If not, do you have time to plan around potential obstacles and think your decision through? Are you prepared to act? As the author writes, "choosing the right time is the most difficult part of the courage calculation; it takes a deep sensitivity to one's surroundings and a great deal of patience."

2. *Do I have sufficient contingency plans?* What is the realistic worst-case scenario? Can you live with those consequences, should they come to pass?

IN MY OWN LIFE

OWNING THE PAST AND EMBRACING THE FUTURE

During a *Where Leadership Begins* seminar that I was delivering, I met Trent. Inspired by the session, Trent decided to choose courage, take a risk, be vulnerable, and pursue a leadership role he had previously avoided for no clear reason and every reason he could think of. After the first day, Trent approached me to share what he had done. His story illustrates that vulnerability in leadership isn't about revealing weakness; rather, it's about building trust, taking responsibility, and inspiring others through vulnerability and authenticity. Here is Trent's story.

Trent sat at his laptop, knowing that what he was about to write would take more than confidence—it would take courage, authenticity, and a deep sense of vulnerability. His hands hovered above the keyboard, hesitating momentarily as doubt crept in. He had made mistakes in the past, and now was the time to confront them. Yet, he knew that true leadership meant being open—not just about his strengths but also about where he had faltered.

Trent's career is a testament to his unwavering dedication and expertise in the HVAC contracting industry. From his early college days, through the challenge of running and selling his own business, to his current role at Advantage Mechanical, he has left an indelible mark on every aspect of the business. His extensive experience has given him a profound understanding of the landscape, the customers, the employees, and even the competitors. However, despite his vast knowledge, he acknowledges that something has gone wrong in recent years. He had allowed his focus to drift, prioritizing commercial sales over the broader managerial responsibilities of his role. The financial impact had been significant, and the results were disappointing. Still, he knew it wasn't just his failure—it was a breakdown in leadership across the board.

As Trent composed the email to the leadership team, he knew it couldn't be a typical self-promotional pitch. If he wanted to earn their trust and move forward as General Manager (GM) for Texas, he had to do something more powerful: acknowledge the truth, take responsibility, and show them his strengths and vulnerabilities.

He began the email with care, knowing how important it was to strike the right tone.

Email Excerpt:

Gentlemen,

I have been giving the GM position consideration over the last several days. I know this may come as a possible surprise to this change of heart towards my continued leadership at Advantage Mechanical.

Trent paused. He wasn't just offering a professional opinion—he was opening up about his change of heart, revealing that even someone with his experience could wrestle with uncertainty. By admitting this, he demonstrated that leadership wasn't just about knowing all the answers but also about being willing to reconsider, learn, and grow. I am committed to this growth and to earning your trust.

He continued by laying out his qualifications, not out of arrogance, but with conviction. He wanted to communicate his readiness to lead the Texas operation. Yet, the real heart of the message came when he owned the department's recent struggles.

Email Excerpt:

In the past few years, I took my eye off the ball on the managerial side and focused on commercial sales only. That was our department's downfall and our past and current GM's mismanagement. The past years' financials were not properly appropriated and accrued in the year of the project's revenue. This $250K was pulled right from the bottom line... That was not a Trent failure. That was a management failure.

Trent knew this admission was risky. Leaders often shy away from acknowledging mistakes, especially when seeking advancement. Yet here he was, taking responsibility without placing all the blame on himself. By owning his part and sharing his learning, he demonstrated vulnerability—not as a weakness but as a way to foster accountability and trust.

He didn't stop at reflecting on the past. Instead, Trent pivoted to focus on what could be done differently moving forward. He outlined a bold plan for rebuilding the commercial department, focusing on maintenance—a strategy he knew from experience would feed future sales growth. His message was clear: mistakes had been made, but he had learned from them, and he had a plan to ensure the department thrived again.

Email Excerpt:

Moving forward, I feel that I have the complete package and then some as my leadership skills continue to grow. Under my leadership, we will develop our sales department with a renewed focus on maintenance, and simply put, that business model has always been successful in feeding replacement sales.

Trent's vulnerability extended beyond admitting mistakes. In his closing lines, he asked a difficult question: did the organization believe in him enough to invest in his leadership? While confident in his ability to lead the team, he acknowledged the risk from the company's perspective.

Email Excerpt:

My only concern is not that I cannot handle these demands but that Advantage Mechanical can afford to have me in the driver's seat. If you think about it, it's an investment in our future, allowing us to grow quickly and make these achievements a reality... I know it's been weighing on your minds how you're going to get this Texas market up and rolling quickly. I'm your answer. Please consider me as your next GM.

Trent hit "send" on the email with a sense of relief. Regardless of the outcome, he knew that he had spoken his truth. He had owned his past, articulated his value, and placed himself vulnerably before the leadership team. The ball was now in their court, but Trent understood something crucial: leadership is not about projecting perfection. It's about showing up authentically, admitting mistakes, and having the courage to embrace vulnerability.

By sending that email, Trent had already taken the first step toward his envisioned future. Whether or not the leadership team chose him for the role, he knew he had acted with integrity. His choice to embrace courage and vulnerability had given him the power to move forward as a leader and a better version of himself.

Lessons from Trent's Vulnerability

Trent exemplified the power of authenticity and vulnerability by acknowledging his mistakes, sharing his personal growth, and offering a solution for the future. His email wasn't just a pitch for a job—it was an act of courageous leadership, setting the stage for a renewed chapter in his career.

This story reminds us that leadership begins when we stop pretending to have all the answers and start showing up as authentic, flaws and all.

Moral Courage

Let's take a moment to talk about the second of these "courage calculations," determining the importance of your goals. Sometimes the "hard" decision is not very hard at all — for example, while most leaders might find the prospect of firing a direct report difficult, it's significantly easier if they have a long, documented history of insubordination, or if you catch them loading up their personal van after hours with expensive office equipment. In these cases, the hard action of termination is softened somewhat by the alignment of your personal values and the interests of the organization.

But what if your supervisor asks you to commit to an action that doesn't make sense (like the IMOL Leader Coaching story from Chapter 1), and your attempts to point out the flaws in their logic fall on deaf ears? Or if your supervisor asks you to do something that violates your personal morals, or to "look the other way" if you witness an action that violates company policy (or basic right vs. wrong)?

In her article "Moral Courage: A Virtue in Need of Development?," Lachman defines[101] moral courage as "the individual's capacity to overcome fear and stand up for his or her core values":

It is the willingness to speak out and do that which is right in the face of forces that would lead a person to act in some other way. It puts principles into action. Physical harm could be a threat in cases of moral courage; however ... this personal sacrifice often is accompanied by a sense of peace because the individual stood up for a non-negotiable principle.

Another study calls it[102] "...speaking up for what is right even when opposition exists; and acting upon conviction despite facing an unpopular environment." It harkens back to our requirements of courage, acknowledging the repercussions of failure but proceeding because you believe the action is necessary, important, and right. The courageous decision is entirely founded upon your core values and principles, which means it could potentially run counter to the values and principles of the organization (take a moment to revisit your values from the Values Discovery exercise from Appendix 2).

Chances are, at some point in our lives, we were presented with a moment requiring moral courage, where the right decision required some level of risk or jeopardy, physical or otherwise. As you might imagine, this kind of discomfort is something you can become acquainted with intimately in the Army.

IN MY OWN LIFE:

"THE ICEMAN"

Starting in December 2005, I was stationed at Camp Liberty, which was just west of the Baghdad International Airport, on the west side of Baghdad. As I previously shared, we did not have an initial mission. When we did finally secure one we were charged with providing food and logistics support for an operation in Camp Rustamiyah, roughly six miles southeast of Sadr City, on the far east side of Baghdad (over 20 miles from Camp Liberty).

Baghdad in 2006 was quite literally a warzone. We were battling an incredible uptick in IEDs and insurgent attacks (notably in Sadr City just North of Rustamiyah), and we were stationed not far from those who sought to do us harm. (For context, in the decade following my time in Iraq, Camp Liberty was the site of two major mortar attacks that killed 30 people and wounded more than 100.) Driving through Baghdad was not something to be taken lightly: For security purposes, logistics and combat patrols move at night, when there is less traffic on the roads and with advanced technology, we have a superior ability to maneuver. Considering the landscape of the city, there were lots of high-rise buildings that provided cover for sniper and rocket attacks, plus you had to drive slowly enough to spot any IEDs on the road before you triggered them. So even though both camps were in Baghdad, each trip from Camp Liberty to Camp Rustamiyah took over an hour and had a high potential for danger or death.

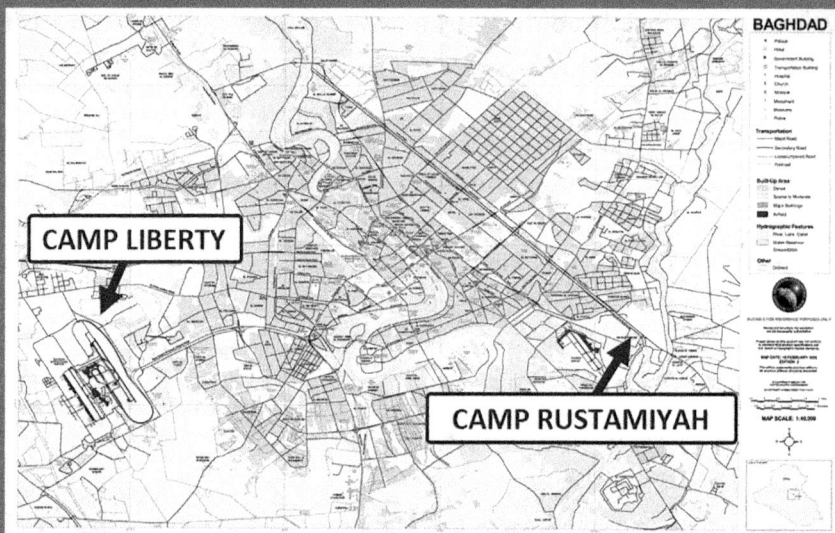

In the summer of 2006, my commanding officer informed me that the units operating out of Camp Rustamiyah had run out of ice for their upcoming combat missions, and he charged me with replenishing their supply of ice. Being out of ice was a major problem for the soldiers stationed there, especially in the heat of the summer.

However, this was a major logistical challenge for two major reasons:

- When Iraq is depicted in the movies as being sunny, dry, and hot, I can tell you this portrayal is 100% accurate. In the summer of 2006, we were working in 120°F heat. Even at night it stays in the 100s.

- Camp Liberty didn't have refrigerated ("reefer") trucks or containers that could transport anything cold let alone ice.

Aware of our soldiers' need for ice, I personally wanted nothing more than to find a way to get it to Camp Rustamiyah. However, after my team and I spent several hours trying to secure refrigerated trucks or containers without success, I had to return to my boss and inform him that we could not transport the ice.

My commanding officer refused to accept this outcome. He then ordered me to investigate transporting pallets of ice on a military truck called a palletized loading system (PLS).

Now, I am not a scientist, but even I understand that when ice is exposed to hot air, it melts. Even driving at night, any ice we put on a palletized loading system would be water before we were even a mile out of camp. But when I explained the problem to my commander, I was told to "figure it out" and to get that ice to Camp Rustamiyah ASAP.

By nature, logistics officers are problem-solvers — and again, I very much wanted to deliver this

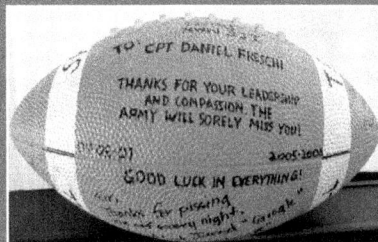

much-needed ice to our combat soldiers. But this mission was futile, and even attempting to carry out my commander's orders would put our soldiers in harm's way. (And for no reason, because the ice would never have made it — we would have arrived in Camp Rustamiyah with nothing as it would have evaporated in the heat.)

So, I did the only thing I could do — I told my commander no.

Now, refusing a direct order is not something that will get you far in your Army career. And while my commanding officer ultimately chose not to write me up for insubordination, there was a clear breach in trust between the two of us. But I also earned the gratitude of the soldiers in my care who didn't have to risk their lives for a pointless mission.

This story is concluded in the Afterword.

Oftentimes, the right decision is the hard one. One blogger on leadership talks[103] about the courage leaders need to have to stand up for what they know is right:

When was the last time you stood up for what you believed in? When did you VOICE an opinion that was contrary to what the majority of other people were saying? When have you taken a risk and did something new: a new skill, a new activity, or a new behavior?

How did this make you feel? Scared? Excited? Uncomfortable? Satisfied? It was probably a combination of all those feelings and a few more mixed in there. What was the outcome? Allow yourself to feel all those emotions — you cannot control that — but do not let fear determine the outcome.

Do you want to follow or lead? Do you want to remain quiet when you should speak up? That's what courageous leadership is about: taking small, baby steps into the unknown, making yourself known, giving your opinion, asserting your feelings for what you believe is right, having an impact — having a VOICE.

When faced with that kind of decision, it might be easy to defer to organizational hierarchy (with the rationalization that the higher-up "knows best"), to show that you're a team player, or to choose not to act "in the best interests of the shareholders." Before making that decision, it might be worth thinking through what it would mean:

- *It signals complicity.* You've no doubt heard some version of a saying by Reverend Charles Aked: "It has been said that for evil men to accomplish their purpose, it is only necessary that good men should do nothing" — or, more succinctly, "what you tolerate you teach." By not acting to stop the behavior, you only encourage it in the future. You enable it and become part of the problem.

- *It demonstrates weakness.* Instead of standing up to what you know is wrong, you're showing you don't have the courage of your convictions — that you know the difference between right and wrong, but you don't have the fortitude to live it in action.

- *Perhaps most importantly, it shows a lack of leadership.* If leadership were easy, everyone would do it, and there wouldn't be a need for leadership coaches. Leadership is hard, and it requires making hard decisions, including standing up for what is right even when doing so is unpopular. The principled stand is rarely the easy decision, but it's often the right one.

If nothing else, there are practical reasons for not tolerating unprincipled behavior: Were it to come to light, your action — or inaction — would be viewed as part of the problem.

In an instance like this, you may have other options that meet the goals of the organization and don't violate your values. These are worth exploring, so long that they're not used as an excuse to avoid doing the right thing. (It's also worth remembering that values are not always black or white: You may find that they can evolve as time passes, as the context evolves, as you gain more experience, and as you mature as a leader and a human.)

As a leader, as a bringer of change, you need to ask yourself what kind of organizational culture you want to foster. Leadership is rarely about doing the minimum to stay on the right side of your compliance department — it's far more commonly aligned with exhibiting professional moral courage. In fact, one could argue[104] that building moral strength and helping people throughout the organization respond to challenges with courage is the only way to shape your company's ethical culture and achieve peak organizational performance.

Doing the right thing can take courage, especially if it means standing up to those higher in the organization or risking the spite of your peers. Ultimately, it's what good leaders do.

Choice Theory and Courage

You'll recall the distinction Glasser makes between choice theory and control theory. With control theory, you use external coercion (threats, promises, force, if necessary) to get someone else to do what you want. With choice theory, you replace what Glasser calls[2] "this ancient I-know-what's-right-for-you tradition" with a new paradigm based on cooperation and trust:

This book is all about this human toll and how it can be reduced by both learning why external control is so harmful and how a new, pro-relationship theory can replace it. ... As we attempt to do this, we will continually ask ourselves: Will what I am about to do bring me closer to these people or move us further apart? How we use this basic question and what would be possible if we did are the heart and soul of this book.

This approach to interacting with others — asking *Will what I am about to do bring me closer to these people or move us further apart?* — applies to all relationships, including those in the workplace:

What prosperity we have had has been due to the fact that besides their strong need for power, most people who have become successful also have a strong need for love and belonging. They built a lot of their success on good relationships with the people they do business with and the people who work for them. ... Once you give up external control psychology for choice theory, it is almost impossible for you to come into contact with people who work for you and not think about how much better it would be if we all got along well. If these contacts are satisfying, it feels good, and you will tend to want even better relationships; that's how our genes work.

As leaders (or aspiring leaders), we know this to be true: We get better effort and performance from those we are personally connected to, and who are personally connected to us, than we do from those who are solely motivated by money or hierarchical power. We also know that at times there's going to be tension between the leader and the led: As we discussed previously, for these or any relationship to succeed, participants have to give up some of their autonomy for the greater good. In those times, it's worth remembering your primary role as a leader.

More than anything else, leaders are charged with maintaining quality-world relationships with the people they lead. Yes, leaders need to have an awareness of evolving circumstances outside of the organization, but your primary responsibility is keeping the people you lead motivated and engaged as those circumstances change. When you strip away the bravado that typifies the popular culture view of what it means to be a leader, what you're left with is that leading is primarily about building relationships with and caring for those you've been asked to or chosen to lead.

Let me share with you a real-life example. One company I worked with liked to have its leaders also be revenue generators, where half the time they are watching out for their teams but the other half they are focused on bringing in more clients. At the same time, one of their top priorities was recruiting and especially retaining their top talent. I strongly advised that if they valued leaders and their relationships as much as they claimed, they would make the leadership role a full-time job — and compensate them accordingly. They declined to take on this initiative, and continued to consider leadership as an add-on to money-making. To this day, they still struggle with higher turnover rates — and were even sued by someone they hired to recruit for them. As a result, they continue to spend more time (and money) to bring new people in and try to build new relationships from scratch. If nothing else, it's inefficient and ultimately counterproductive.

Building Relationships Through Courage

> *"Family isn't always blood. It's the people in your life who want you in theirs, who accept you for who you are. The ones that would do anything to make you smile and who love you no matter what."*
> — *John R. Freschi, Sr.*

So the question becomes: How do you build the kinds of leadership relationships that foster employee engagement? The answer: The way you build all your other important relationships — with courage.

Whenever you have an organization of people pursuing some greater goal, leadership is primary and essential. (Don't get me started on "leaderless teams." Seriously — don't! It pains me.) Making sure the people in your organization are engaged and focused on their tasks is your primary goal, and the ability to build and maintain relationships is, in my eyes, the true test of leadership.

Going back to our definition of courage as the median between hope and fear, as a leader you form your business (and personal) relationships with the hope of engagement, care, and personal commitment from those you lead. You don't want people in your organization working just for a paycheck or some other motivation — you want them to be inspired. You want them to care about and love what they do. And for that to happen, you have to show that you care, that you love them, that you yourself are personally invested in them.

Even if that means acknowledging your flaws and mistakes.

Even if that means sharing things about yourself you'd rather keep hidden.

Even if that means speaking out on things that matter to you, no matter how unpopular.

Even if that means shifting the spotlight off of you and onto your team.

And even if that means risking rejection or getting removed from someone else's quality world.

Have the courage to be self-aware, to be authentic, to be vulnerable, and to be humble. These things may not come naturally for you, and that's OK. Courage can be taught and developed. As one researcher noted[100]:

In business, courageous action is really a special kind of calculated risk-taking. People who become good leaders have a greater than average willingness to make bold moves, but they strengthen their chances of success — and avoid career suicide — through careful deliberation and preparation. Business courage is not so much a visionary leader's inborn characteristic as a skill acquired through decision-making processes that improve with practice. In other words, most great business leaders teach themselves to make high-risk decisions. They learn to do this well over a period of time, often decades.

Other researchers on leadership reached[105] a similar conclusion:

But moral courage is not merely an automatic behaviour per se; it is a practice, consistently doing what one knows one ought to do. This is central to human flourishing because, as individuals struggle with their desires and reasoning, sustained fortitude helps them to overcome their own internal strife. Moral courage is a consistent practice of having the virtue of willpower.

So yes, courage can be taught — courage can be practiced — courage can even become a habit. It starts with a leader who is willing to take the initiative to choose courage, and to begin the courageous journey.

That is where leadership begins.

Are you ready to choose?

AFTERWORD

There are two final points I'd like to make about leadership and choice theory, but before we get to that, I wanted to take a moment to thank you for spending a few hours with this book and exploring where leadership truly begins.

If there's one guiding principle I hope you take away from our time together, it's that leadership starts with you — with how you choose to act, behave, think, and respond. Once you understand that key point, that *your success as a leader is under your control,* then you can start to take steps toward becoming the leader you want to be. That's the crux of my coaching practice — guiding new, developing, and even seasoned leaders to realizing and seizing the opportunity before them. To make the choice to change and be better than they ever imagined.

Everyone's leadership journey begins at different points in their lives. Some start by accident, some by crisis, some by choice. However you started, it is the choice to get better as a leader every day that will separate you from others. It's a choice to learn about those you lead. It's a choice to embrace the characteristics we discussed and act on them that will leave a legacy — your legacy — with others.

Look at the five leadership characteristics we discussed in this book:

- self-awareness

- authenticity

- humility

- vulnerability

- courage

It might be easy to infer a direct correlation between these characteristics and effective leadership: "If I become more vulnerable, or if I become more courageous, I'll be a better leader." While that can be true, it's not strictly a two-part equation, or a direct line leading from vulnerability to leadership, or courage to leadership.

There is a missing and crucial component in all those possible equations.

Take a look at what one study had to say about increasing your self-awareness[106]:

Introspection, the act of looking within, helps you lead with trust. Knowing yourself makes it possible to adjust to people and situations, facilitates empathy by making it easier to relate to others and be related to, and paves the way for more rewarding working relationships.

It's about *trust* — it's always been about trust. It's about building strong relationships with those whom you've been charged to lead. If you look closely at these five characteristics, you'll see that all of them have the result of creating closer relationships with the people you interact with. Whatever you can do to increase the levels of trust among the members of your team will only increase your team's effectiveness and satisfaction. To quote Glasser[2]:

Lead managers know that the core of quality is managing workers so they put the manager; each other; the work; the customers; and, in private industry, the stockholders into their quality worlds. That is, all who are involved must get close and stay close.

Adele Lynn, author of *The EQ Difference*, wrote[107] that our internal world drives how we interact and respond to our world, our quality world. These leadership choices will help you develop stronger emotional intelligence, which in large part is about our internal world. When you examine these choices, you begin to understand and work towards achieving your life's purpose.

At the end of the day, leadership is about your followers, not about you. Leadership begins when you've made the choice to learn enough about yourself to cross the threshold into the quality worlds of others. You would be amazed at what a team can accomplish when they trust each other and their leader.

The second point I wanted to emphasize is that all five of these leadership elements require you to make a choice. They don't just happen. You don't "pick up" vulnerability through experience as a leader. You have to consciously choose to be vulnerable. You have to practice it! It's a skill that can be developed, if you're willing to put in the time and effort.

I've coached leaders from all over the country, from mid-level team leads up to CEOs. While they each had their own leadership styles and concerns, they all *chose* to improve their relationships with their teams and become better leaders.

I hope you succeed on your leadership journey. I'd love to hear how it goes — email me at Iknow@whereleadershipbegins.com.

IN MY OWN LIFE:

THE REST OF THE STORY

When I shared episodes from my own life, I hope they illustrated how these different components of where leadership begins, existing not in the abstract but from my lived experiences. Still, some may be wondering what happened after those stories ended.

At the **intervention with my mom**, she ultimately did acknowledge her drug use and eventually chose to go into rehab. After a challenging time, she emerged clean and sober and remained clean and sober for over ten years, a considerable accomplishment. Unfortunately, shortly after I returned from Iraq, her father and my grandfather passed away from esophageal cancer. He was diagnosed while I was deployed and vowed to make it until I returned, and he did. His passing put her into a tailspin of bad choices that reintroduced drugs and alcohol back into her life. We could not endure the emotional toil she would leech from us, and despite several attempts to help her, we as a family made a tough decision to remove her from our quality world. Now, our choices have consequences, namely questions from our kids, but we've been able to leverage the examples she's offered us to help them shape their quality worlds and instill better influences in their lives (primarily my Aunt Pam).

After 15 years of absence and as this book was being written, my mother was reintroduced into my quality world. While not strictly at the center, she has returned due to recent health and legal issues I have chosen to help with.

Due to the squalor and hoarding conditions she has been living in, cognitive issues due to a previous stroke, and head injury due to a fall, she recently fell again inside her home and broke her ankle. The break required surgery and placement in a rehabilitation hospital for recovery.

In March 2023, I had to make a choice, was I going to let her continue to spiral out of control and burden others or was I going to help lessen the burden on others by bringing her back to my quality world? I chose to lessen the burden.

Over my spring break, I flew to California for eleven days and partnered with my younger sister Michelle to permanently remove her from the squalor conditions she was living in. Through the medical evaluation process, we also learned that she would never be able to live independently again and would need to move into an assisted living environment with significant help.

Over those eleven intense days, Michelle (who has kept our mom in her quality world intermittently) and I worked diligently to establish an estate plan, power of attorney, and other legal documents to unravel her life and reconstitute it in a comfortable way where her basic needs are being met.

The best part of this choice was that I could reintroduce my younger sister, Michelle, her kids, and her husband back into my quality world and my family's quality world and us into theirs. Michelle and I grew up together for many years and suffered much disappointment and sadness due to our mother. We were always trying to help our mom clean her life up literally and figuratively. But at some point, you find enough needles and drugs and must choose to move on to take care of your own family. And we did, in our way, work to use our mother as a model of what we never wanted to become. Both Michelle and I pray this will be our final attempt to put her on a healthy and productive path to live out the remainder of her life comfortably.

A few months after the first edition of *Where Leadership Begins* was published, my **Aunt Pam** passed away from health-related complications. My Aunt Pam outlived the life expectancy of a person who sustained the injury she did, and she made the most of every single day she had here. As you can see, my Aunt Pam has been an extraordinary person in my life and my family's life, and she has been that same person in many of her students' and families' lives. This was evident by the thousands of tributes made on Facebook from generations of people she impacted daily through her teaching.

My Aunt Pam was a selfless champion for others in her daily life - always positive, always present, always the cheerleader, and always smiling.

Pam's beacon of light shined on everyone who crossed paths with her. This light must continue and be shared by many future generations, which is why I decided to launch The Pam Courtney Foundation Memorial Fund. The Pam Courtney Foundation has been established to continue her legacy in the College Glen and Hubert H. Bancroft communities.

The Pam Courtney Foundation is in its early stages, and it has been such an honor and a privilege to support the community she selflessly committed herself to for many decades and across multiple generations.

The Pam Courtney Foundation Memorial Fund exists to help offset the costs of membership fees for families that play sports in the College Glen community, such as soccer clubs and Little Leagues; Support the talent show financially at Hubert H. Bancroft in the Sacramento City Unified School District; and in the future, provide annual scholarships to Hubert H. Bancroft graduates pursuing higher education in education, sports management, or arts-related fields to support their efforts to pursue a given aspiration.

So far in our first year, we have been able to support the Bancroft PTO in many events, sponsor the renaming of the community little league tee ball field, sponsor the local swim team, sponsor the local soccer club jamboree, and many other events.

Soon, we will publish a series of ten children's books titled "Miss Pam's Here!" to tell fun stories about my Aunt Pam's time as the extraordinary teacher and person she was to so many.

We would love for you to support our mission by donating.

You can learn more by visiting our Facebook page or our foundation website:

www.facebook.com/PamCourtneyFoundation

www.pamcourtneyfoundation.org

In my story about **why I wear cowboy boots**, I mentioned working with a recruiting firm to begin my civilian career. After my work with them, I was not only hired to do something I felt was natural for me, but I also came back and recruited additional junior military officers (JMOs) for the company that hired me using that same recruiting firm—but sitting on the other side of the table.

I had a unique perspective because I sat on the same side of the table as the JMOs I was now interviewing. I could help them navigate the typical interview questions to get authentic answers. When I had a junior military officer in front of me, I asked them to set aside the canned response because I knew what they were trained to say and suggested they relax and share an authentic answer. It helped many officers who were nervous going into the interviews, and we hired many of them who showed their true, authentic selves in the hiring process.

The recruiting firm that helped me transition is an outstanding company that provides tremendous help to JMOs transitioning into corporate America. The JMO recruiting firm is a business that places JMOs in large companies for 25-30% of the candidate's first-year contracted salary. While nothing is inherently wrong with this business model, they provide an excellent service to JMOs and the companies we ultimately get hired to work for.

They helped me immensely, and I am grateful for their guidance and support. I don't know where I'd be today if I hadn't used them in my transition. Most JMOs who used their process transitioned into roles consistent with or related to what they did in the military. For example, during my transition, they set up interviews with companies seeking logistical or operations roles. I had offers for logistics roles from Cardinal Glass, Carrier, Valspar, and Bolthouse Farms, but logistics is not what I had my heart set on. I felt I was called to and wanted to develop leaders. It just so happened that a company was looking for a leadership development instructor at my hiring conference. It was a perfect match for me.

Nevertheless, I believe that JMO candidates should never compromise their true selves while searching for answers to important interview questions. Being as authentic as possible is more important and less stressful because your authenticity gap is smaller.

After I **decided to leave the Army,** I ultimately "went corporate" before starting my leadership development and executive coaching practice. Still, while the story was focused on my choice to leave, I wasn't the only one who made that choice. Three other company-grade officers under the same leadership also decided to leave the service. They were "top box" quality staff officers who served alongside me, and the reason they cited for leaving the military was the unit's senior leader's poor decisions. Two of us joined our state's national guard units for a short period, but that was to serve out the remainder of our obligated contract time. I want to reiterate that I love the military, I am a proud veteran, and I do not regret one moment of my time in service to this country. I wish that the senior leaders made better decisions in many aspects, many that I've chosen not to reveal here but still cause reflection, frustration, and pause as I consider my time in the Army. Perhaps I was too idealistic when I entered the military, that I had too high of expectations of my leaders but wouldn't you if you were leading America's sons and daughters into war.

After being let go, how did **EDGE** come about? EDGE is an acronym, something the military taught me to make, and stands for Extraordinary Development, Growth Exponentially. I started EDGE about two months after being let go from my first post-military job. I started EDGE because, in 2010, there were very few prospects of available jobs in my field due to the market conditions and I didn't want to settle for something I wasn't passionate about — and I knew I'd need to provide for my family. Soon after I acquired my first client, I received a call from a local financial services firm looking for a Talent Development Consultant. After a few interviews, I was hired in June. Through an agreement, they allowed me to keep EDGE up and running, and I was able to provide my services to them and service my clients at the same time. My business grew over the four years I worked for the financial services firm and eventually I was able to step out on my own completely. As of 2025, EDGE celebrates its 15th anniversary. You can read more about EDGE at the end of the book.

The **Fox River Bandits**' approach to **baseball** is simple: We focus on the fundamentals of throwing, catching, hitting, and fielding. We aim to help youth players grow and develop baseball and life skills while contending against quality competition. We utilize the best coaching to teach and play the correct fundamental baseball.

We are not an academy and do not provide a year-round baseball experience. We support youth development in multiple sports to increase their versatility as they approach high school.

Our goal at the end of the day is to provide a fun and competitive baseball experience and help to prepare the athlete to learn to love the game, the lessons it offers life, play the game for as long as they want to and prepare them to compete for and earn a spot at the high school level.

Our focus is on competing and learning, win or lose

As for **Dan Gaynor,** well, shortly before the first edition of this book was published, he was inducted into the Wisconsin Baseball Coaches Association Hall of Fame and received the 2022 Distinguished Service Award, the highest honor one can obtain (aside from a Hall of Fame induction) for his contributions to the sport of baseball.

His humble service to the community is unmatched. He's coached many of the coaches in our program and continues to develop our youth in baseball. Coach Gaynor still plays softball with his friends and coaches at the local high school.

DAN GAYNOR- MILWAUKEE AREA

Dan Gaynor has coached various high school sports for close to 50 years. He was the Head Baseball Coach at Omro High School back in 1970. Dan was the Head Baseball Coach at West Allis Central from 1993-2007. From 2009-2022 Dan has been an Assistant Coach at both Waukesha South and Waukesha West. Dan has also done many volunteer coaching roles, including Mike Hegan Baseball Camps, AAU Winter Camps, RTE Travel Baseball, (which included a La Crosse *Stars of Tomorrow Open Division Championship*), and the West Allis-West Milwaukee Recreation Department. Under Gaynor's leadership as head coach, Wisconsin's AAU Teams have reached the National Tournament twice.

Because of Coach Gaynor's impact on me, other Bandits' coaches, and many young athletes, we have an annual "Dan Gaynor Award." The essence of this award is for the athlete who has been the best teammate. An athlete who is selfless and understands that it's not about individual stats but instead about the team and puts their team before all else. They know that whether they are on the bench or the field, they have an essential role as a teammate.

An athlete who has regularly demonstrated this quote from Coach Gaynor:

"If you are not fielding the ball, you're covering a base. If you're not covering a base, you're backing someone up. If you're not backing someone up or moving on the field, you're up in the dugout cheering

for your team. You always have a job to do! If you want to be a spectator, buy a ticket."

Martha. While Martha's story was mostly focused on summoning courage and overcoming her fears, there is a little more to include. About one year into Tina's tenure, Martha's organization was supervising a retreat that coincided with her maternity leave. Because this annual event was community-run and Martha had meticulously planned every detail of the organization's (limited) involvement, she felt comfortable with Tina managing that year's event unsupervised and even letting her husband volunteer to help out. We later discovered that Tina disregarded many of Martha's carefully planned instructions and used the organization's funds to pay her husband without authorization. Tina also billed the organization for 40 hours per week during Martha's maternity leave instead of the agreed-upon 30 hours per week, even though the extra hours were neither warranted nor authorized. All told, Martha accumulated 13 pages of documentation spelling out Tina's problematic behavior, and that was enough to overcome the organization's nonconfrontational and permissive culture to proceed with her dismissal.

My "Iceman" story has a funny coda. A few days after the initial order, we could secure the refrigerated trucks, deliver the much-needed ice, and replenish their rations. To this day, I think about this mission order and how it was handled. It was one more reason for me to leave the military. If leaders were going to continue to issue these directives in the future and not learn from them, how could I, in good conscience, choose to stay? We were not supposed to be there in the first place, and on top of that, to execute a mission that was destined to fail was simply poor leadership, not to mention dangerous. As a result of this standoff between me and my commanding officer, I earned the nickname "Iceman" as a term of endearment, and for the remainder of our tour we adopted the theme song "Cold as Ice" by Foreigner for my commander. If you listen to the lyrics, it's very fitting.

What's with the football? The football or MECC Ball was part of a care package we had received from a family we knew back home. The football became a symbolic hand-off between shifts, between the SPOT Team who planned the combat logistics patrols and the Fusion Cell who was responsible for monitoring the missions. I was responsible for leading both teams while in Iraq. On evenings when we didn't have a mission, we'd play catch with it. Many things were broken as a result, but it sure was a great time and one that I will cherish forever. The two teams provided me with the ball as a going away gift signed by all who were in my care. This plastic football happens to be one of my most cherished possessions. They let me into their quality worlds, and for that, I am forever grateful.

APPENDIX 1
DEFINING YOUR QUALITY WORLD

Glasser suggests that a person's quality world consists of a small collection of specific images representing the best ways to fulfill our basic needs. These images can be categorized into three groups: (1) the people we most desire to be with, (2) the things we most wish to own or experience, and (3) the ideas or belief systems that largely guide our behavior.[2]

What people, experiences, or beliefs contribute to your quality world? You can list them below, alongside examples from my own life.

People We Most Want To Be With

(Example: My son)

Things We Most Want To Own or Experience

(Example: Coaching my son's baseball team)

Ideas of Systems of Belief That Govern Most of Our Behavior

(Example: A better relationship due to a shared passion)

Defining and understanding the people and things that are most important to you can help you sort through your feelings and behaviors, as a person and a leader.

Who or what are you already excluding from your quality world?

Why are you excluding these items from your quality world? Are you excluding them because they add no value or because you want to avoid an authentic (but challenging) conversation?

Are there any people, activities, things, ideas, or places that you feel you may need to exclude from your quality world? Why?

APPENDIX 2
VALUES DISCOVERY

Throughout my time here on Earth, I have learned that we must decide who we want to be before deciding what we want to do.

In *Principles: Life and Work*, Ray Dalio reinforces[108] the idea that we must have a set of leadership principles to help us understand who we are as leaders. He asserts these principles must:

- Be formed from personal values for ourselves

- Be based on a foundation of
    - beliefs
    - experiences
    - backgrounds
    - goals
    - our nature to serve

- Provide a framework that guides our daily choices and leadership
    - in our community
    - at work
    - in our lives

When we make choices and determine actions based on our values, we can respond more efficiently and effectively to situations while maintaining our values' integrity.

In examining your values, it's helpful to understand that we have **programmed values** and **developed values**. Programmed values are those we've consistently acted upon over time without any real conscious thought about our belief in the value. Developed values differ in that they are a choice, formed freely, through direct experience with the object of the belief, examination of the alternatives, and anticipation of potential consequences. These values are more thorough and therefore considered a more conscious representation of your values.

Values are essential in your approach to choosing to lead. They are an enduring belief that a particular end or mean is preferable to a different end or mean. Essentially, your values are what you choose to consider to be essential or not important. One author contended[109] that individuals possess the same amount of values to a large extent but to different degrees. Mostly everyone values peace, for example, but some choose to make it a higher priority than others.

Perhaps more important, however, is the perception your direct reports hold of your values. Their perceptions of what you value profoundly influence their motivation, confidence, and choice to follow you. To lead others effectively, it's critical to clearly define what values you hold and establish a baseline for how others perceive your values.

Your values are qualities or characteristics that you value. You would sooner leave an organization or step down as a leader than violate your values. Your values guide your intentions, and they influence how you lead. When your values are clear and you are conscious of them, you create a solid foundation for leadership.

Consider the following criteria when examining your own developed, chosen values:

1. **Freely Chosen:** The value is a cognitive choice you make yourself, with an absence of subtle or overt influence. This means you have had the chance to evaluate the underlying belief source and have consciously chosen the practical and suitable value for you.

2. **Chosen From Alternatives**: Choosing a value based on the knowledge that it is the most significant choice against two or more alternatives. It is essential to give thoughtful consideration as to why you've chosen a specific value.

3. **Chosen After Considering Consequences**: A developed value requires examining each alternative for its positive and negative consequences. The value requires a choice, and a choice involves reflection.

4. **Acted Upon Over Time**: The chosen value is acted upon and part of your regular behavior patterns (a single act does not constitute a value but is a good start). As a leader, it would be inauthentic and to claim a specific value without reliably modeling the value and demonstrating it over time.

5. **Prized and Publicly Owned**: If you have a chosen, genuine value, then you are willing to acknowledge it publicly and enthusiastically. You could test your choice of value against others' perception, and if confronted, you wouldn't deny it.

So, what are your values? What do you value? Before proceeding, I recommend you spend some time pondering these questions. I've developed a Values Discovery card sort that will guide you to assist in this process — as you go through cards and think about your choices, you might be surprised by the results. I only ask that you remain open-minded and allow the process to work.

Values Discovery

Instructions:

1) Shuffle and then lay out all the values cards (the ones with the big words and definitions on them) so you can see all of them.

2) In a nearby space, place the five category areas, left to right:

    a. Value Always (the values that matter most to you)
    b. Value Often
    c. Value Sometimes
    d. Value Rarely
    e. Value Never (the values that matter least to you)

Note: For this process to deliver benefits to you, you must approach it authentically and truthfully. There are no right or wrong, or good or bad, choices here. The only way to sabotage the process is to attempt to be someone you are not, especially when you make a choice you feel is more socially acceptable or what you think other people expect of you, regardless of whether the value is true for you. Remember, it is just you and a deck of cards — you have nothing to fear from being honest.

3) Read each value card carefully, both the value and the definition. At first, the values and definitions may appear redundant, but some nuances make them different. These nuances are essential as you think about what you value.

4) After considering the nuances, internalizing, and considering each value card's concepts and context, begin to place them in one of the five category areas.

5) Once you have sorted all the cards into one of the categories, prioritize the top 5–10 "Value Always" cards from the most to least important, asking yourself, "What values are indisputable?" It might be necessary to add some cards from a closely related category such as Value Often or Sometimes. These then are the values you discovered and should revalidate against the criteria.

6) Referring to the Value Rarely and Value Never categories, ask yourself, "What is it about the values that I never consider and why?"

APPENDIX 3
EXPLORING AUTHENTICITY

This checklist provides actionable steps for leaders to embrace authenticity. **Authentic leadership** means aligning your actions with your values, being transparent, and leading with integrity. Authenticity is a continuous process that involves aligning your actions with your values, being transparent in your communication, and **staying true to yourself, especially in challenging times**. Committing to authenticity creates an environment where **trust flourishes** and your team can thrive under your leadership.

Use this checklist to evaluate how you show up as a leader and find opportunities to foster greater authenticity to close your authenticity gap in your daily work and as a tool for **self-reflection and growth**.

1. Know and Align with Your Core Values
   o Have I identified my personal values?
   o Do I regularly reflect on how my actions align with those values?
   o Have I shared my values with my team to promote transparency?
   o Am I acting in ways that reflect both my personal values and the organization's mission?

2. Lead with Integrity
   o Do I make decisions consistent with my values, even under pressure?
   o Have I communicated my expectations and commitments to others?
   o Do I follow through on promises, even when it's challenging?
   o Am I honest and transparent about difficult decisions?

3. Foster Open Communication and Transparency

- o Do I communicate openly with my team, sharing successes and challenges?
- o Am I willing to admit when I don't have all the answers?
- o Do I encourage open dialogue and invite input from others?
- o Have I created a space where team members feel comfortable sharing their thoughts and concerns?

4. Be True to Yourself

- o Am I leading in a way that reflects who I truly am, or am I trying to fit into someone else's leadership expectations?
- o Do I avoid pretending to be perfect or infallible in front of my team?
- o Am I comfortable expressing my authentic opinions and ideas, even when they differ from others?
- o Do I show consistency between my words and actions, maintaining integrity across different situations?

5. Embrace Vulnerability

- o Am I open about the challenges and uncertainties I'm facing?
- o Do I model learning by admitting mistakes and sharing what I've learned?
- o Have I asked for help when needed, showing that relying on others is okay?
- o Am I willing to give honest, constructive feedback and receive it in return?

6. Build Authentic Relationships

- o Do I take time to understand my team members personally?
- o Am I fostering trust by being honest and transparent with my colleagues?
- o Do I express genuine appreciation and give credit where it's due?
- o Have I demonstrated empathy by recognizing my team's individual needs and experiences?

7. Stay True During Difficult Times
- o When facing tough decisions, do I stay aligned with my values rather than compromising for convenience?
- o Do I handle conflicts with honesty and openness?
- o Am I willing to have uncomfortable conversations when necessary to maintain trust and integrity?
- o Do I remain consistent in my leadership, even under stress or uncertainty?

8. Encourage Authenticity in Others
- o Have I encouraged my team members to bring their whole selves to work?
- o Do I celebrate the diversity of thought and respect different perspectives?
- o Have I provided opportunities for others to share their unique ideas and insights?
- o Do I model authentic behavior, inspiring others to be open and genuine?

9. Reflect and Evolve Continuously
- o Do I regularly reflect on whether I stay true to my authentic self?
- o Have I sought feedback from trusted colleagues on my leadership authenticity?
- o Am I willing to adjust if I notice that I'm straying from my values or trying to please others?
- o Do I embrace growth as part of authenticity, knowing authenticity is a lifelong journey?

10. Balance Confidence with Humility
- o Am I confident in my strengths without becoming arrogant?
- o Do I share my achievements without diminishing the contributions of others?
- o Have I remained open to learning, acknowledging that I don't know everything?
- o Do I practice humility by actively listening to others and valuing their input?

Based on this checklist, what does it say about my authenticity gap? Do I have a large authenticity gap? Where is the tension coming from?

APPENDIX 4
EXPLORING HUMILITY

Some individuals may possess a natural inclination toward humility, but for most, it is a practice that requires deliberate effort. As discussed in the book, humility is a choice that must be actively integrated into leadership behaviors. Below are some ways leaders can practice humility in their work:

1. **Ask for Help and Welcome Feedback:**
    Humble leaders are unafraid to **ask for support** and **actively seek team feedback.** They create a culture of openness where others feel safe sharing ideas and constructive criticism.

2. **Admit Mistakes and Learn from Them:**
    Acknowledging mistakes without defensiveness and **forgiving others** for their errors helps build trust and promotes a culture of continuous learning. Leaders like Maria (from the Preface) demonstrate humility by **owning their missteps** and using them as growth opportunities.

3. **Adopt a Growth Mindset:**
    Humble leaders understand that there is always more to learn. They seek new experiences, embrace different perspectives, and encourage their team to do the same. They see challenges as invitations for growth, not threats to their status.

4. **Prioritize the Needs of the Team:**
    Humility in leadership means prioritizing the team's success and well-being over personal recognition. Leaders practice servant leadership by removing obstacles for their team, offering support, and celebrating their achievements.

5. **Model Inclusive Leadership:**
   Humble leaders foster inclusivity by ensuring that every voice is heard and valued. They know that the best solutions come from diverse ideas, and they welcome collaboration across all levels of the organization.

6. **Give Credit Where It's Due:**
   Leaders who embody humility share credit generously. Instead of seeking personal praise, they highlight the contributions of their team members and celebrate collective success. This builds a culture of mutual respect and appreciation.

7. **Commit to Lifelong Learning:**
   Humble leaders recognize that leadership is a journey, not a destination. They are committed to their development and regularly engage in activities that expand their knowledge and skills.

Pursuing humility requires a journey of self-awareness, authenticity, and growth in emotional intelligence. Humility is about acknowledging our imperfections and recognizing that we are humans leading other humans. It encompasses pursuing excellence while staying grounded, embracing our true selves, inspiring others, and remaining open to their knowledge and experiences.

Choose to be self-aware. Identify your strengths and weaknesses and learn to appreciate the diversity that defines who you are. By quieting your ego and listening deeply—with every part of your being—you create a profound space for understanding and empathy.

Choose to be authentic. Have the courage and integrity to show your true self and genuinely empathize with others. In moments of openness and vulnerability, you can learn powerful lessons and discover a deeper connection with your fellow human beings.

Choosing to be humble is a lifelong journey intricately woven through your experiences, emotions, and interactions with others. A genuine understanding of humility fosters peace, personal growth, and deeper connections, enriching your heart with the beauty of human experience.

Take a moment to journal your thoughts on choosing to be humble and humility.

Where and when are you demonstrating humility now?

Where can you develop more humility in your leadership and life?

Who are role models of humility in your life that you can emulate and learn from?

What is preventing you from choosing to be humble?

APPENDIX 5
EXPLORING VULNERABILITY

In addition to the three examples of where I messed up (By All Means, Let's Write a Book), I have one last one that still holds today. In one of the leadership courses I developed, I asked my participants about vulnerability, asking them, "Why would anyone want to be led by you?" During the course, the participants then spent reflection time uncovering the answer to this question. I felt I should do the same since I asked them to answer this question. Here is my response, straight from my leadership journal:

Why would anyone want to be led by me?

> *Anyone would want to be led by me because I do what I say I will do. I inspire others towards a vision of shared sacrifice. I enable and encourage others to be themselves. I take risks and challenge others productively to take risks and reward great effort regardless of success or failure. Anyone would want to be led by me because I am accountable for my behavior and willing to hold others accountable for theirs. I am generous with my expectations and even more so in my feedback. I am incredibly thankful for others' feedback, encouraging and asking for it often to develop stronger relationships. I am willing to support others' ideas even if they don't work out, never suppressing their creativity.*
>
> *I want to help people learn from their mistakes and experiences, such as mine, by offering grace and forgiveness to maximize their potential and allow them to soar.*

As a leader, being insecure about my stories and past missteps brings me a feeling of shame, but hiding behind these insecurities and shame prevents me from growing and learning. To close out this peek behind the curtain, let me ask you: Where can you take a risk to be more vulnerable in your life? Open your Johari Window wider to develop stronger relationships and reveal your authentic self. Answering "Why would anyone want to be led by you?" is a great place to start.

Self-awareness is understanding who you are and how you are similar to and different from others. This understanding helps be vulnerable with others. If you do not understand yourself, it is nearly impossible to share yourself with others. If you've not taken time to examine your past experiences and learn, it will be challenging to develop vulnerability.

Personal reflection is an excellent way to raise your level of self-awareness and engage in vulnerability.

Reflection helps you uncover yourself through inquiry. You can set aside daily time to consider your successes, challenges, feelings, and relationships. Rather than just doing things because you always have, ask yourself what behaviors contribute to successes and challenges and what feelings drive you and your relationships.

Review the following checklist to examine behaviors that could increase your level of vulnerability.

Ways to Be More Vulnerable

This checklist emphasizes that vulnerability involves building trust, fostering connections, and enhancing team performance rather than indicating weakness. Leaders are encouraged to balance openness, growth, and responsibility effectively.

1. **Admit Imperfections and Mistakes**
   o Openly acknowledge mistakes in front of the team.
   o Frame errors as opportunities for learning rather than failures.

2. **Ask for Help and Input**
   o Seek advice or help from team members when facing challenges.
   o Involve others in decision-making to foster collaboration.

3. **Share Personal Struggles When Appropriate**
   o Share relevant personal challenges to humanize your leadership.
   o Balance professional distance with emotional openness.

4. **Practice Self-Awareness and Humility**
   o Reflect regularly on your strengths and areas for improvement.
   o Use feedback as a growth opportunity and model self-improvement.

5. **Model Emotional Honesty**
   o Express emotions (e.g., stress or uncertainty) constructively.
   o Show that it's okay not to have all the answers.

6. **Foster Psychological Safety**
   o Encourage team members to ask questions and share concerns.
   o Make it safe for others to admit mistakes without fear of punishment.

7. **Develop Genuine Connections with Others**
   o Build personal relationships with team members based on mutual respect.
   o Show genuine interest in their well-being beyond their roles.

8. **Demonstrate Courage in Conversations**
   o Be willing to have difficult conversations with empathy and authenticity.
   o Approach conflicts with openness to resolve issues together.

9. **Lead by Example**
   o Take small risks by sharing vulnerabilities with trusted colleagues first.
   o Gradually expand your openness as you build trust.

10. **Balance Vulnerability with Leadership Accountability**
   o Show vulnerability while maintaining confidence and decisiveness.
   o Ensure your openness aligns with the mission and team dynamics.

After reviewing these behaviors, where could you increase your level of vulnerability? You don't have to do it all at once. That would be overwhelming, so where could you start to gain some early wins for yourself?

Consider journaling your thoughts daily and reviewing them weekly or monthly to identify recurring themes. This practice can enhance your self-awareness by revealing your underlying motivations.

Since my time in the Army, I have used this journal to document my thoughts on leadership. It contains many concepts and ideas for this book.

Consider starting your journaling process and reflect on why anyone should choose to be led by you.

APPENDIX 6
COURAGEOUS DECISION GUIDE

Questions to Ask Before Making a Courageous Decision:

1. **What are my goals?** Determine if your goals are attainable, ethical, and moral.

2. **How important are my goals?** A courageous choice involves personal and professional risk. Before committing to it, ask yourself if the goal is worth the risk.

3. **Do I have a supportive power network?** How strong are your relationships with your direct reports, peers, and other influencers within your organization?

4. **What are the trade-offs?** See the matrix on Pages 195-196 for more questions.

Refer to the table on Page 195-196.

Other Questions to Considers Before Making a Courageous Decision:

- **Is now the time to act?** Is this an emergency? If not, do you have time to plan around potential obstacles? What would happen if you delayed the decision until later?

- **Do you have sufficient contingency plans?** What is the realistic worst-case scenario? Can you live with those consequences? Should they come to pass?

- **Will your decision bring you closer to your people or move you further apart?**

- **Have previous similar decisions led to successes or failures?**

- **Should you solicit feedback and ideas from others in the company before making the decision?**

Take a moment to reflect on an action, conversation, career move, personal commitment, or any situation where you may need to act courageously.

Where is courage needed but often avoided in my life, work, or organization?

What are the reasons I avoid exercising more courage?

What benefits might arise from demonstrating more courage in my life, work, or organization? What drawbacks might exist?

What does courage look like when I demonstrate it?

REFERENCES

You might be surprised to learn that this book is not the only book anyone has written about leadership. (I know that's hard to believe, but it's true.) I wanted to pursue this because the idea that leadership is a *choice* — that everything we do is a choice, that we are responsible for our own successes and failures and our own happiness — is a topic not often discussed when considering what it takes to be a leader.

I highly recommend that everyone — aspiring leader or not — check out William Glasser's *Choice Theory: A New Psychology of Personal Freedom* and other works. It might give you insight into becoming a better leader and becoming a better person.

Here are the other resources I used in putting together this book:

[1]Harding, A. S. (2004). *Two Generals Apart: Patton and Eisenhower.* Military History Online. Available at: https://www.militaryhistoryonline.com/wwii/articles/twogeneral.aspx.

[2]Glasser, W. (1998). *Choice Theory: A New Psychology of Personal Freedom.* New York: HarperCollins Publishers.

[3]Glasser, W., & Glasser, C. (1998). *The Language of Choice Theory.* New York: HarperCollins Publishers.

[4]Gallup, Inc. (2019). *The Engaged Workplace.* Available at: https://www.gallup.com/services/190118/engaged-workplace.aspx.

[5]*The LMJ.* (2014, August 18). *Lesson From Deming: Drive Out Fear; Create Trust.* Available at: https://the-lmj.com/2014/08/lesson-from-deming-drive-out-fear-create-trust/.

[6]Hougaard, R., et al. (2018, January 29). Why Do So Many Managers Forget They're Human Beings? *Harvard Business Review*. Available at: https://hbr.org/2018/01/why-do-so-many-managers-forget-theyre-human-beings.

[7]Eurich, T. (2018, January 4). What Self-Awareness Really Is (and How to Cultivate It). *Harvard Business Review*. Available at: https://hbr.org/2018/01/what-self-awareness-really-is-and-how-to-cultivate-it.

[8]Hixon, J. G., and Swann Jr., W. B. (1993). When Does Introspection Bear Fruit? Self-Reflection, Self-Insight, and Interpersonal Choices. *Journal of Personality and Social Psychology*, 64(1), 35-43.

[9]Stanford Encyclopedia of Philosophy. (2019, October 18). Introspection. Available at: https://plato.stanford.edu/entries/introspection/

[10]Guthrie, D. (2012, August 9). Creative Leadership: Introspection. Available at: https://www.forbes.com/sites/dougguthrie/2012/08/09/creative-leadership-introspection/#2a37f4662d68.

[11]Fuller, D. (2015, June 23). Leadership Insights — Introspection Is Key to Growth and Development. Available at: https://www.linkedin.com/pulse/leadership-insights-introspection-key-growth-debbie-fuller

[12]Esposito, J. L. (2002). *What Everyone Needs to Know About Islam: Answers to Frequently Asked Questions, From One of America's Leading Experts*. New York: Oxford University Press.

[13]Prichard, S. (2015, June 23). What Type of Leader Are You? Available at: https://www.skipprichard.com/what-type-of-leader-are-you/.

[14]Boot, A. (2016, February 7). Leadership Introspection: The Only Person You Can Actually Change Is Yourself. Available at: https://leadershipwatch-aadboot.com/2016/02/07/leadership-introspection-the-only-person-you-can-actually-change-is-yourself/.

[15]Eurich, T. (2017, June 2). The Right Way To Be Introspective (Yes, There's a Wrong Way). TEDx. Available at: https://ideas.ted.com/the-right-way-to-be-introspective-yes-theres-a-wrong-way/.

[16]Sedikides, C., et al. (2007). The Why's the Limit: Curtailing Self-Enhancement With Explanatory Introspection. *Journal of Personality,* 75(4), 783-824.

[17]Sze, D. (2017, December 6). The Limits of Introspection. The Huffington Post. Available at: https://www.huffpost.com/entry/introspection-research_b_7306546.

[18]Grant, A. M., et al. (2002). The Self-Reflection and Insight Scale: A New Measure of Private Self-Consciousness. *Social Behavior and Personality,* 30(8), 821—836.

[19]Young, S., et al. (2018). Give Your Leaders a Developmental Edge: The Power of Digitally Enabled Assessments. Center for Creative Leadership. Available at: https://www.ccl.org/wp-content/uploads/2018/08/give-your-leaders-developmental-edge-white-paper-CCL.pdf.

[20]Heathfield, S. M. (2019, April 23). Core Values Are What You Believe. The Balance Careers. Available at: https://www.thebalancecareers.com/core-values-are-what-you-believe-1918079.

[21]Kanter, R. M. (2010, May 3). Adding Values to Valuations: Indra Nooyi and Others as Institution-Builders. *Harvard Business Review.* Available at: https://hbr.org/2010/05/adding-values-to-valuations-in.html.

[22]Loepp, B. (2017, October 23). VIDEO: Dr. Hogan Discusses the Importance of Values. Hogan Assessments, The Science of Personality. Available at: https://www.hoganassessments.com/video-dr-hogan-discusses-importance-values/.

[23]Lichtenstein, S. (2012, January). The Role of Values in Leadership: How Leaders' Values Shape Value Creation. *Integral Leadership Review*. Available at: http://integralleadershipreview.com/6176-the-role-of-values-in-leadership-how-leaders-values-shape-value-creation/.

[24]Center for Creative Leadership Labs (2020). CCL Labs survey: we need more trust, less executive image! Available at https://cclinnovation.org/cclresults-the-competencies-for-future-success/

[25]Kraemer, H. B. J., Jr. (2011, April 26). The Only True Leadership Is Values-Based Leadership. *Forbes*. Available at: https://www.forbes.com/2011/04/26/values-based-leadership.html#ad47573652b7.

[26]Reed, G. (2019, Winter). Focus on the Locus: A Response to "The Rhetoric of Character and Implications for Leadership". Available at: https://jcli.scholasticahq.com/article/7523-focus-on-the-locus-a-response-to-the-rhetoric-of-character-and-implications-for-leadership-by-george-reed

[27]Ibarra, H. (2015, January-February). The Authenticity Paradox. *Harvard Business Review*. Available at: https://hbr.org/2015/01/the-authenticity-paradox.

[28]Fuda, P., and Badham, R. (2011, November). Fire, Snowball, Mask, Movie: How Leaders Spark and Sustain Change. *Harvard Business Review*. Available at: https://hbr.org/2011/11/fire-snowball-mask-movie-how-leaders-spark-and-sustain-change.

[29]Walumbwa, F. O., et al. (2010). Psychological processes linking authentic leadership to follower behaviors. *The Leadership Quarterly,* 21, 901-914.

[30]Lehman, D. W., et al. (2018). Authenticity. *Academy of Management Annals,* 13(1). Available at: https://www.researchgate.net/publication/327276702_Authenticity.

[31]Trilling, L. (1972). *Sincerity and Authenticity*. Cambridge, Massachusetts: Harvard University Press.

[32]Michie, S., and Gooty, J. (2015). Values, Emotions, and Authenticity: Will the Real Leader Please Stand Up? *The Leadership Quarterly,* 16, 441-457.

[33]Center for Creative Leadership. (2022). Lead With That: What Betty White and Sidney Poitier Can Teach Us About Inclusion, Access, and Authenticity. Available at: https://www.ccl.org/podcasts/lead-with-that-what-betty-white-and-sidney-poitier-can-teach-us-about-inclusion-access-and-authenticity/.

[34]Robinson, S., and O'Dea, V. (2017). Authentic Leadership — To Thine Own Self Be True. Available at: https://www.insights.com/media/1107/authentic-leadership.pdf.

[35]Schepici, K. (2011, November 3). Introspection as a Pathway to Authentic Leadership. Linkage, Inc. Available at: http://blog.linkageinc.com/blog/introspection-as-a-pathway-to-authentic-leadership.

[36]Avolio, B. J., et al. (2004). Unlocking the Mask: A Look at the Process by Which Authentic Leaders Impact Follower Attitudes and Behaviors. *The Leadership Quarterly,* 15, 801-823.

[37]Schrier, J. (2017, April 24). The Courage It Takes To Be Authentic in Building Your Practice. Available at: https://thepracticefreedommethod.com/the-courage-it-takes-to-be-authentic-in-building-your-practice/.

[38]Elrod, D. J. (2012, August). The Importance of Being Authentic. Strategic Finance, Institute of Management Accountants. Available at: https://sfmagazine.com/wp-content/uploads/sfarchive/2012/08/LEADERSHIP-The-Importance-of-Being-Authentic.pdf.

[39]Vlachoutsicos, C. (2012, December 7). What Being an "Authentic Leader" Really Means. *Harvard Business Review.* Available at: https://hbr.org/2012/12/what-being-an-authentic-leader-really-means.

[40]Coughlin, C. (2016, May 5). Leaders: Do You Know Why You Want to Lead? Center for Higher Ambition Leadership. https://www.higherambition.org/leaders-know-want-lead/.

[41]Hogan Assessments. (2019). RELEVANT Releases Article on Humility and New Leadership. Available at https://www.hoganassessments.com/relevant-releases-article-on-humility-and-new-leadership/.

[42]Merryman, A. (2016, December 8). Leaders Are More Powerful When They're Humble, New Research Shows. *The Washington Post.* Available at: https://www.washingtonpost.com/news/inspired-life/wp/2016/12/08/leaders-are-more-powerful-when-theyre-humble-new-research-shows/.

[43]Bobb, D. J. (2013). *Humility: An Unlikely Biography of America's Greatest Virtue*. Nashville, Tennessee: Thomas Nelson, HarperCollins Christian Publishing.

[44]Lindsay, D. (2018). Views From the Field: Humble Leadership. An Interview With Edgar and Peter Schein. *The Journal of Character & Leadership Development.* Available at https://www.usafa.edu/app/uploads/JCLD-Fall2018-Press_webfinal_new092018.pdf.

[45]Kusch, R., Hogan, R., Sherman, R., and Czernik, A. (2019). Our View on New Leadership: How To Grow Humility in Charismatic Leaders. RELEVANT Management Consulting. Available at https://relevant-mb.de/download/Assessing_and_Developing_Humility.pdf.

[46]Chancellor, J., & Lyubomirsky, S. (in press). Humble beginnings: Current Trends, State Perspectives, and Hallmarks of Humility. Social and Personality Psychology Compass. Available at: http://sonjalyubomirsky.com/files/2012/09/Chancellor-Lyubomirsky-in-press.pdf.

[47]Peters, G. (1999—2021). Final Presidential Job Approval Ratings. *The American Presidency Project.* Ed. John T. Woolley and Gerhard Peters. Santa Barbara, California: University of California. Available at: https://www.presidency.ucsb.edu/statistics/data/final-presidential-job-approval-ratings.

[48]Goodwin, D. K. (2008). Lessons From Past Presidents. TED2008. Available at: https://www.ted.com/talks/doris_kearns_goodwin_lessons_from_past_presidents?language=en

[49]Prime, J., and Salib, E. R. (2014). Inclusive Leadership: The View From Six Countries. Catalyst, Inc. Available at: http://www.catalyst.org/knowledge/inclusive-leadership-view-six-countries.

[50]University of Buffalo. (December 9, 2011). Humility Key to Effective Leadership. *ScienceDaily.* Available at: www.sciencedaily.com/releases/2011/12/111208173643.htm.

[51]Bullwinkle, K. (2015, December 8). What Is Humble Leadership? Talent Gear. Available at: https://www.talentgear.com/learn/january-2016/humble-leaders/.

[52]Deffler, S. A., et al. (2016). Knowing What You Know: Intellectual Humility and judgments of recognition memory. *Personality and Individual Differences,* 96 (2016): 255-259.

[53]Ou, A. Y., Waldman, D. A., & Peterson, S. J. (2018). Do Humble CEOs Matter? An Examination of CEO Humility and Firm Outcomes. *Journal of Management,* 44(3), 1147—1173. Available at: https://doi.org/10.1177/0149206315604187.

[54]Shaffer, G. (2020). Look for the Helpers: Humble Leadership in Times of Crisis. Hogan Assessments. Available at: https://www.hoganassessments.com/look-for-the-helpers-humble-leadership-in-times-of-crisis/.

[55]Chima, A., and Gutman, R. (2020). What It Takes to Lead Through an Era of Exponential Change. *Harvard Business Review.* Available at https://hbr.org/2020/10/what-it-takes-to-lead-through-an-era-of-exponential-change.

[56]Dee, L. (2014, March 21). Al Haig and the Reagan Assassination Attempt — "I'm in Control Here." Association for Diplomatic Studies & Training. Available at: https://adst.org/2014/03/al-haig-and-the-reagan-assassination-attempt-im-in-charge-here/.

[57]McLean, S. (2020). Coronavirus: How to Survive and Thrive. Markstein, April, 1-6. Available at: https://markstein.co/wp-content/uploads/2020/04/COVID-19_How-to-Survive-Thrive_WhitePaper.pdf.

[58]Grande, D. (2018). The Imperative of Humble Leadership. *American Nurse Today,* 13(3). Available at: https://www.americannursetoday.com/imperative-humble-leadership/.

[59]Feldman, K. L. (2008, Winter). Chick-fil-A's Second Generation Aims To Go 'the Second Mile.' *Family Business*. Available at: https://www.familybusinessmagazine.com/chick-fil-second-generation-aims-go-second-mile-0.

[60]Warren, R. (2014, September 9). Chick-Fil-A Founder Truett Cathy Truly Lived His Faith. *Time*. Available at: https://time.com/3310038/rick-warren-chick-fil-a-founder-truett-cathy-truly-lived-his-faith/.

[61]Goudreau, J. (2015, March 24). The CEO of Popeyes Says Becoming a 'Servant Leader' Helped Her Turn Around the Struggling Restaurant Chain. *Business Insider*. Available at: https://www.businessinsider.com/popeyes-ceo-servant-leadership-traits-2015-3.

[62]Miller, H. L. (2022, May 11). Former CEO of Popeyes Used Servant Leadership to Save the Company. Leaders.com. Available at: https://leaders.com/articles/leaders-stories/cheryl-bachelder/.

[63]Bachelder, C. (2016, September 6). Humble and Confident Leadership? Is That Possible? Serving Performs With Cheryl Bachelder. Available at: https://www.cherylbachelder.com/humble-and-confident-leadership-is-that-possible/.

[64]Prime, J., and Salib, E. R. (2014). The Best Leaders Are Humble Leaders. *Harvard Business Review*. Available at: https://hbr.org/2014/05/the-best-leaders-are-humble-leaders.

[65]Hu, J., et al. (2018). Research: When Being a Humble Leader Backfires. *Harvard Business Review*. Available at: https://hbr.org/2018/04/research-when-being-a-humble-leader-backfires.

[66]Sugarman, J., et al. (2011). *The Eight Dimensions of Leadership*. Oakland, California: Berrett-Kohler Publishers, Inc.

[67]DDI. (2020, December 2). Why Executives Fail: 3 Common — and Avoidable — Pitfalls. Available at: https://www.ddiworld.com/blog/why-executives-fail-3-common-and-avoidable-pitfalls.

[68]Sherman, R. A. (2018). Humility, Leadership, and Organizational Effectiveness. Available at: https://trainingindustry.com/articles/leadership/humility-leadership-and-organizationaleffectiveness/.

[69]Schein, E. H. (2018). *Humble Leadership: The Power of Relationships, Openness, and Trust.* Oakland, California: Berrett-Koehler Publishers.

[70]Seppala, E. (2014, December 11). What Bosses Gain by Being Vulnerable. *Harvard Business Review*. Available at: https://hbr.org/2014/12/what-bosses-gain-by-being-vulnerable.

[71]Brown, B. (2012). *Daring Greatly: How the Courage To Be Vulnerable Transforms the Way We Live, Love, Parent, and Lead.* New York, New York: Penguin Group (USA), Inc.

[72]Brown, B. (2010, June). The Power of Vulnerability. Available at: https://www.ted.com/talks/brene_brown_on_vulnerability

[73]Johnson, C. Y. (2015, October 15). The Wildly Hyped $9 Billion Blood Test Company That No One Really Understands. *The Washington Post*. Available at: https://www.washingtonpost.com/news/wonk/wp/2015/10/15/the-wildly-hyped-9-billion-blood-test-company-that-no-one-really-understands/.

[74]Patrick, A. (2022, January 14). Elizabeth Holmes May Be a Fraud, But She Knows Leadership Psychology. *Financial Review*. Available at: https://www.afr.com/work-and-careers/management/elizabeth-holmes-may-be-a-fraud-but-she-knows-leadership-psychology-20220112-p59nm3.

[75]Randazzo, S., et al. (2022, January 3). The Elizabeth Holmes Verdict: Theranos Founder Is Guilty on Four of 11 Charges in Fraud Trial. *The Wall Street Journal*. Available at: https://www.wsj.com/articles/the-elizabeth-holmes-verdict-theranos-founder-is-guilty-on-four-of-11-charges-in-fraud-trial-11641255705.

[76]Malone, M. (2021, September 15). Theranos Trial Highlights the Dark Side of Leadership. University of Miami, News @ the U. Available at: https://news.miami.edu/stories/2021/09/theranos-trial-highlights-the-dark-side-of-leadership.html.

[77]Thier, J. (2022, May 7). JPMorgan and Goldman Sachs Are Monitoring How Often Employees Are Coming Into the Office — but Experts Say That Approach Could Backfire. Fortune.com. Available at: https://fortune.com/2022/05/07/companies-are-tracking-how-often-employees-are-coming-to-the-office/.

[78]Polzer, J. (2018). How Showing Vulnerability Helps Build a Stronger Team, by Daniel Coyle. Available at: https://ideas.ted.com/how-showing-vulnerability-helps-build-a-stronger-team/.

[79]Brendel, D. (2014, July 22). Expressing Your Vulnerability Makes You Stronger. *Harvard Business Review*. Available at: https://hbr.org/2014/07/expressing-your-vulnerability-makes-you-stronger.

[80]Lencioni, P. (2018). What Makes a Team Cohesive? The Five Behaviors of a Cohesive Team. Available at: http://www.fivebehaviors.com/About.aspx.

[81]Bunison, G. (2020, May 10). Special Edition: It's Time to Be Vulnerable. Personal Communications. Korn-Ferry. Available at: https://maximizebusinessmarketing.com/email-from-gary-burnison-korn-ferry-ceo.

[82]Brown, B. (2013, June 6). Brené Brown's Advice on Vulnerability: 6 Types of People to Never Confide In (VIDEO). Available at: https://www.huffingtonpost.com/2013/06/06/brene-brown-advice-vulnerability_n_3392414.html.

[83]Razzetti, G. (2018, September 18). How To Move From Fear to Fearlessness. Ladders, Inc. Available at: https://www.theladders.com/career-advice/how-to-move-from-fear-to-fearlessness.

[84]Curzer, H. J. (1996, December 28). "Aristotle's Account of the Virtue of Courage in Nicomachean Ethics III.6-9." Binghamton University, The Society for Ancient Greek Philosophy Newsletter. Available at: https://orb.binghamton.edu/cgi/viewcontent.cgi?article=1182&context=sagp.

[85]Harris, H. (1999). Courage as a Management Virtue. *Business and Professional Ethics Journal,* 18(3&4), 27-46.

[86]Koerner, M. M. (2014). Courage as Identity Work: Accounts of Workplace Courage. *Academy of Management Journal,* 57(1), 63-93.

[87]Voyer, P. (2011, November/December). Courage in Leadership: From the Battlefield to the Boardroom. *Ivey Business Journals.* Available at: https://iveybusinessjournal.com/publication/courage-in-leadership-from-the-battlefield-to-the-boardroom/.

[88]Parkinson, M. (2017, March 8). Be Bold Enough To Be Introspective for Change. *The Sydney Morning Herald.* Available at: https://www.smh.com.au/opinion/be-bold-enough-to-be-introspective-for-change-on-international-womens-day-20170308-gut9jd.html.

[89]Baggett, J. (2018, March 26). Integrity and Courageous Authenticity: Why Being True to Who You Are and Speaking Up Matter in Leadership. Catchlight Consulting LLC. Available at: http://www.wecatchlight.com/integrityandauthenticity/.

[90]Brown, B. (2016, June 5). My Response to Adam Grant's *New York Times* Op/ED: Unless You're Oprah, 'Be Yourself' Is Terrible Advice. LinkedIn. Available at: https://www.linkedin.com/pulse/my-response-adam-grants-new-york-times-oped-unless-youre-bren%C3%A9-brown/.

[91]Tardanico, S. (2013, January 15). 10 Traits of Courageous Leaders. *Forbes.* Available at: https://www.forbes.com/sites/susantardanico/2013/01/15/10-traits-of-courageous-leaders/#45f7dfac4fc0.

[92]Shellenbarger, S. (2018, Oct. 9). The Best Bosses Are Humble Bosses. *The Wall Street Journal.* Available at: https://www.wsj.com/articles/the-best-bosses-are-humble-bosses-1539092123.

[93]Hogan Assessments. (2018, Oct. 15). A Q&A on Humility. Hogan Assessments. Available at: https://www.hoganassessments.com/a-qa-on-humility/.

[94]Pearse, S. (2017, May 29). Courage, The Most Important Leadership Virtue. The Huffington Post. Available at: https://www.huffingtonpost.com/susan-pearse/courage-the-most-importan_b_10186426.html.

[95]George, B. (2017, April 24). Courage: The Defining Characteristic of Great Leaders. Available at: https://www.forbes.com/sites/hbsworkingknowledge/2017/04/24/courage-the-defining-characteristic-of-great-leaders/#6b0feb8a11ca.

[96]Godin, S. (2008). *Tribes: We Need You to Lead Us.* London: Penguin Books Ltd.

[97]Goulston, M. (2006). *Get Out of Your Own Way at Work … and Help Others Do the Same: Conquer Self-Defeating Behavior on the Job.* New York: Perigee Trade.

[98]Treasurer, B. (2015, Sept. 13). Courage Is the Key to Great Leadership. Entrepreneurs' Organization. Available at: https://www.eonetwork.org/octane-magazine/special-features/courageisthekeytogreatleadership.

[99]Lomenick, B. (2013, April 30). Six Ways To Be a More Courageous Leader. Available at: https://www.fastcompany.com/3008966/6-ways-to-be-a-more-courageous-leader

[100]Reardon, K. K. (2007). Courage as a Skill. *Harvard Business Review,* 1, 1-7.

[101]Lachman, V. D. (2007, April). Moral Courage: A Virtue in Need of Development? Ethics, Law and Policy. *MEDSURG Nursing*, 16(2), pp. 131-133.

[102]Gentry, W. A., Cullen, K. L., and Altman, D. G. (2012). "The Irony of Integrity A Study of the Character Strengths of Leaders." The Center for Creative Leadership. Available at: https://www.ccl.org/wp-content/uploads/2015/04/IronyOfIntegrity.pdf.

[103]Larsen, P. (2014). Courageous Leadership: Step Out of Your Comfort Zone to Make an Impact. Emergenetics International. Available at: https://www.emergenetics.com/blog/courageous-leadership/.

[104]Sekerka, L. E. (2014, March 3). Building Moral Courage as a Professional Practice. Available at: https://www.researchgate.net/publication/228486143_Building_Moral_Courage_as_a_Professional_Practice.

[105]Sekerka, L. E., and Bagozzi, R. P. (2007, April). Moral Courage in the Workplace: Moving to and From the Desire and Decision To Act. *Business Ethics: A European Review,* 16(2), 132-149.

[106]Green, C. H., and Howe, A. P. (2011). *The Trusted Advisor Fieldbook: A Comprehensive Toolkit for Leading With Trust.* New York: John Wiley & Sons.

[107]Lynn, A. B. (2005). *The EQ Difference: A Powerful Program for Putting Emotional Intelligence to Work.* New York: Amacom.

[108]Dalio, R. (2017). *Principles: Life and Work.* First Simon & Schuster hardcover edition. New York: Simon and Schuster.

[109]Rokeach, M. (1973). *The Nature of Human Values.* New York: Free Press.

[110]Walumbwa, F. O., et al. (2012). Authentic Leadership Self-Assessment Questionnaire. Available at: https://authenticleadershipblog.files.wordpress.com/2012/07/authentic-leadership-questionnaire.pdf.

[111]Kaiser, R., Sherman, R., and Hogan, R. (2023, March). It Takes Versatility to Lead in a Volatile World. Available at: https://hbr.org/2023/03/it-takes-versatility-to-lead-in-a-volatile-world.

[112]Robinson, E. (2024, February). How Humble Leaders Create Engagement. Available at https://www.hoganassessments.com/blog/how-humility-creates-engagement-humble-leaders-build-trust/

[113]Collins, J. C. (2001). Good to great: why some companies make the leap ... and others don't (1st ed). HarperBusiness.

[114]Clark, T. R. (2020). The 4 stages of psychological safety: defining the path to inclusion and innovation (First edition). Berrett-Koehler Publishers, Inc.

[115]Edmondson, A. C. (2019). The fearless organization: creating psychological safety in the workplace for learning, innovation, and growth. John Wiley & Sons, Inc.

[116]Lagace, M. (2018, November 26). Amy Edmondson on how to make your employees feel psychologically safe: "How To Build a Fearless Organization." Harvard Business School Working Knowledge. https://hbswk.hbs.edu/item/make-your-employees-psychologically-safe

[117]Edmondson, A. and Stachowiak, D. (2019, April 14). "How to Build Psychological Safety, with Amy Edmondson." Episode 404. Coaching for Leaders (podcast. https://www.hbs.edu/faculty/Pages/item.aspx?num=62297

[118]Chamorro-Premuzic, T. (2025, November 9). There Is Nothing Authentic About Authentic Leadership. Forbes. https://www.forbes.com/sites/tomaspremuzic/2025/11/09/there-is-nothing-authentic-about-authentic-leadership/

[119]Pfeffer, J. (2015). Leadership BS : Fixing Workplaces and Careers One Truth at a Time. Harper Business, An Imprint Of Harpercollins Publishers.

[120]Tourish, D. (2023, November 27). The Inauthenticity of Authentic Leadership Theory. International Leadership Association. https://ilaglobalnetwork.org/the-inauthenticity-of-authentic-leadership-theory/

ABOUT EDGE

We are faced with choices every day of our life. Many of us face choices that push us to the edge of our comfort zone. Leadership happens on the edge of our comfort zone. We can decide to sit back and let life happen to us, or we can choose to embrace it and encounter everything that comes our way.

Established in 2010 as a state- and federally-recognized Service-Disabled Veteran-Owned Business, EDGE Business Management Consulting, LLC (EBMC or EDGE) is a leadership and organizational development consulting organization. We create extraordinary workforce development experiences using best-in-class and custom solutions to offer leadership and team development, program implementation and support, personality and psychological assessments, training, talent management, executive, team and leadership coaching, and organizational design and development.

At EDGE, we partner with organizations to push the limits of their comfort zone by designing leadership development strategies to grow talent from all areas. We start by learning your culture and integrating it into everything we do.

Each organization we work with has a unique mission statement, vision, purpose, and most importantly, culture and values. Your approach to developing your leaders should be as unique as you are.

We believe actual leadership development requires more than an off-the-shelf, cookie-cutter approach. It needs a thoughtful and integrated system based on how your organization operates.

EDGE is and can add depth to your organization in many forms. Just ask, and you'll see what we can do.

At the EDGE is where leadership begins.

Our Vision

To help the organizations we serve to maximize their culture through their employees' potential to be top performers and leaders.

Our Mission

Our mission is to serve organizations that desire to advance their culture and cultivate their employees' growth, performance, and leadership through extraordinary human capital development processes.

Values: The Cornerstone of Our Success

Ethical. There is no right way to do a wrong thing. We know organizations that win have unquestionable integrity as their foundation. Our ethical compass guides our integrity and all our activities and decisions.

Dignity. We value and embrace the differences of all people and will provide the utmost respect and dignity internally and externally to our organization.

Giving. Our success is dependent on the success of our employees, community, and clients. We will give back in many forms to increase engagement, loyalty, and values.

Excellence. We value an unrelenting quest for excellence, quality, and transparency to achieve our goals by providing our clients with the highest standard of service. *We win when our clients win.*

Our Solutions

Although many of our solutions are custom-built, we utilize numerous proven resources that deliver results. Visit our website or contact us to discover how we can serve you and your organization.

ABOUT THE AUTHOR
DANIEL C. FRESCHI

Dan has more than two decades of experience in leadership, management, human resources, adult education, employee and team development, coaching, and project management within multiple industries. He has a proven track record of increasing organizational capabilities by creating, customizing, redesigning, implementing, facilitating, and measuring global leadership development and talent management initiatives. Dan focuses individual, team, and organizational energy on leveraging strengths to improve performance and deliver results.

Dan is an Operation Iraqi Freedom combat veteran with eight years of military service in the United States Army as a Multifunctional Logistics Officer (transportation), gaining experience leading soldiers in garrison and combat.

Over the course of Dan's corporate career, he has been responsible for developing, implementing, and monitoring manager and leadership development strategies, systems, practices, and programs across enterprises across the country and the globe.

Additionally, he has been instrumental in developing effective competency-based programs and team and cultural development initiatives.

Dan's academic credentials include a Bachelor of Science degree in Criminal Justice-Law from California State University Sacramento and a Master's degree in Human Relations with a focus on Organizational Leadership from the University of Oklahoma. He also has three years of coursework completed toward his Doctorate in business/consulting psychology.

Dan's credentials and professional certifications include:

- SPHR - Senior Professional in Human Resources
- SHRM-SCP - SHRM Senior Certified Professional
- Certified Body Language Trainer - Science of People
- Criterion-Referenced Instruction Designer
- The Rocket Model of Teamwork
- Learning Systems Master Trainer & Certified Facilitator - DDI
- Leadership Architect Suite
- Celemi Simulations Solution Provider
- Denison Culture & Leadership Consulting Partner

Dan is also an adjunct professor at Carroll University, a local private university based in Waukesha and the first and oldest in Wisconsin. He has taught business courses for nearly a decade in the School of Business, including Organizational Behavior, Human Resources Management, Career Management, Leadership and Personal Effectiveness, Principles of Management, Introduction to Business, and Personal Finance.

Outside of his professional efforts, Dan leads a non-profit (501c3) baseball club, the Fox River Bandits. Leading this organization has been a natural companion to his business, as baseball is a true reflection of life. He helps the club's youth and families develop baseball and life skills such as leadership, accountability, resilience, discipline, communication, and many others.

Dan's passions exist in helping others become the best versions of themselves by assisting them to make choices that encourage them to exercise their free will, leading to more freedom in their lives.

Connect with Dan at:
- www.linkedin.com/in/danfreschi/
- www.whereleadershipbegins.com

RECOMMENDED READINGS TO FURTHER YOUR LEADERSHIP DEVELOPMENT JOURNEY:

Brown, Brené. (2015). **Daring greatly: how the courage to be vulnerable transforms the way we live, love, parent, and lead.** Avery an imprint of Penguin Random House.

Clarke, B. & Crossland R. (2002). **The leader's voice: how your communication can inspire action and get results!** (1st ed.). Select Books.

Clark, T. R. (2020). **The 4 stages of psychological safety: defining the path to inclusion and innovation** (First edition). Berrett-Koehler Publishers, Inc.

Cloud, H., & Townsend, J. S. (2017). **Boundaries: when to say yes, how to say no to take control of your life** (Updated and expanded [edition]). Zondervan.

Covey, S. R., Collins J. C., & Covey, S. (2020). **The 7 habits of highly effective people: powerful lessons in personal change** (Revised and updated. Simon & Schuster). Simon & Schuster.

Curphy, G. J. Nilsen, D. L., & Hogan, R. (2014). **Ignition: a guide to building high-performing teams**. Hogan Press.

Dalio, R. (2017). **Principles**. Simon & Schuster.

Edmondson, A. C. (2019). **The fearless organization: creating psychological safety in the workplace for learning, innovation, and growth.** John Wiley & Sons, Inc.

Ehrmann, J., Ehrmann, P., & Jordan, G. (2011). **InSideOut coaching: how sports can transform lives** (1st Simon & Schuster hardcover). Simon & Schuster.

Frankl, V. E. (1992). **Man's search for meaning: an introduction to logotherapy** (Fourth). Beacon Press.

Glasser, W. (1999). **Choice theory: a new psychology of personal freedom** (First HarperPerennial). HarperPerennial.

Glasser, W., & Glasser, C. (1999). **The language of choice theory** (1st ed.). HarperPerennial.

Holiday, R. (2015). **The obstacle is the way: the ancient art of turning adversity to advantage** (Paperback). Profile Books.

Holiday, R. (2016). **Ego is the enemy**. Portfolio Penguin.

Holiday, R. (2019). **Stillness is the key**. Portfolio/Penguin an imprint of Penguin Random House LLC.

Holiday, R. (2021). **Courage is calling: fortune favors the brave**. Portfolio/Penguin.

Holiday, R. (2022). **Discipline is destiny: the power of self-control**. Portfolio/Penguin an imprint of Penguin

Holiday, R. (2024). **Right thing, right now: good values. good character. good deeds**. Portfolio/Penguin.

Kouzes, J. M., & Posner, B. Z. (2023). **The leadership challenge** (7th ed.). John Wiley & Sons Incorporated.

Lencioni, P. (2005). **The five dysfunctions of a team: a leadership fable**. Jossey-Bass A Wiley Imprint.

Maister, D. H., Green, C. H., & Galford, R. M. (2000). **The trusted advisor** (20th-anniversary edition, Free Press trade paperback edition). Free Press.

McKeown, G. (2020). **Essentialism: the disciplined pursuit of less** (Currency trade paperback). Currency.

Watkins, M. (2013). **The first 90 days: proven strategies for getting up to speed faster and smarter** (Updated and expanded [edition]). Harvard Business Review Press.

Willink, J., & Babin, L. (2017). **Extreme ownership: how U.S. Navy Seals lead and win** (Second). St. Martin's Press.

UNLOCK YOUR LEADERSHIP POTENTIAL GO BEYOND THE PAGES!

Discover tools and resources designed to turn inspiration into action.

Transform Reading into Real-world Impact

You've explored the powerful insights in *Where Leadership Begins* — now it's time to apply them. These exclusive resources are tailored to help you lead with courage, authenticity, and purpose, whether building your career, empowering a team, or transforming an organization.

Where Leadership Begins™ Assessment

What it is: Complete the self-assessment to uncover your unique leadership strengths and growth areas.

Why you'll love it:
- Gain personalized insights into your leadership style.
- Pinpoint actionable growth opportunities.
- Set the foundation for your leadership journey.

Take the assessment and unlock the leader within you!

***Where Leadership Begins* Executive Book Summary**

A concise, high-impact summary designed for busy leaders.

Why you'll love it:
- Get the core takeaways of the book in minutes.
- Perfect for quick refreshers or sharing with your team.
- Make leadership wisdom easily digestible and actionable.

Lead smarter, not harder — grab your summary today!

Where Leadership Begins Book Club Process

What it is: A guided framework to explore the book with your team or peers.

Why you'll love it:
- Build connections and deepen relationships through shared learning.
- Spark meaningful discussions about leadership principles.
- Transform group conversations into actionable strategies.

Start your leadership book club and inspire collective growth!

Where Leadership Begins™ Individual Development Plan (IDP) Form

What it is: A step-by-step tool to create your personalized leadership roadmap.

Why you'll love it:
- Clarify your goals and priorities.
- Design actionable steps to grow as a leader.
- Track your progress and celebrate your wins.

Turn goals into reality with the IDP form!

Leadership Awaits – Take the Next Step

These resources are your key to unlocking the full potential of Where Leadership Begins. Whether you want to lead boldly, inspire your team, or grow with intention, we've got you covered.

Visit https://www.whereleadershipbegins.com/resources to explore all the resources and start your journey today!

BATTLE TESTED™ BY EDGE™: EMPOWERING STUDENT-ATHLETE LEADERS

BATTLE TESTED
MUSCLES | MIND | MORALS

In *Where Leadership Begins*, we explore the foundational principles of leadership: self-awareness, authenticity, humility, vulnerability, and courage. We're taking those principles to the field with Battle Tested™ by EDGE™, a premier leadership and character development program for high school and college student-athletes, their coaches, and athletic directors.

Why Battle Tested™ by EDGE™?
Student-athletes face unique challenges both on and off the field. They need more than physical training to excel—mental resilience, strong character, and practical leadership skills. Battle Tested™ by EDGE™ is designed to:

- **Build Resilience:** Equip athletes to navigate setbacks and thrive under pressure.
- **Develop Leadership Skills:** Foster the ability to lead teams with confidence and integrity.
- **Promote Character Growth:** Instill the values that shape exceptional individuals in sports and life.

What We Offer
1. **Customized Workshops:** Tailored programs focusing on leadership, accountability, teamwork, and mental toughness.
2. **Comprehensive Resources:** Access our exclusive content, including Student-Athlete Leadership Assessment (SALA) and Becoming Uncommon.
3. **Coach & AD Training:** Practical tools to help coaches and athletic directors inspire and develop their teams.

Transforming Potential into Performance

Battle Tested™ by EDGE™ isn't just about creating great athletes—it's about developing uncommon leaders. Our proven methodologies prepare student-athletes to excel in competition, the classroom, and their communities.

Join the Movement

Are you ready to unlock the full potential of your student-athletes and coaching staff? Let's partner to build leaders who impact far beyond the game.

Visit www.battle-tested.us **to learn more and get started with Battle Tested™ by EDGE™ today.**

www.ingramcontent.com/pod-product-compliance
Lightning Source LLC
Chambersburg PA
CBHW071334210326
41597CB00015B/1444